Conversations with JC

listening to my Self

volume 2

High View Publishing
P. O. Box 317
Piermont, New York 10968

Cover and Book Design by Donna Schwartz
Cover Photo by Liz Rose

Printed in the United States of America

ISBN #0-933805-01-2

DEDICATION

To our "little brothers and sisters" everywhere.
We are truly one.

ACKNOWLEDGMENTS

We truly have come to honor the purpose of this section in a book. Acknowledging the love and support that it takes to convert these meditations into a lovely book is done with a great sense of gratitude to:

Arnold Patent, who has consistently appreciated and supported this material being shared, and whose own wisdom and clarity we have drawn from in so many ways. Arnold doesn't just talk about principle. He lives it! More than anyone we know, his commitment to principle is daily translated into caring, supportive acts for a multitude of people;

Donna and Steve Schwartz, whom we lovingly refer to as "the Universe" because they so beautifully and efficiently handle all the details. For us, as the "stewards" of this material, a more ideal relationship could not be had. The support they have given us is incredible. As we requested, they have allowed their gentle sensitivity to guide them on every aspect of the publication—from selection of the type and paper to be used, to selecting the site for the photographs that would capture our mental image of the high rock where we meditate and listen to JC's words. They just seem to intuitively know what we want and manifest it exactly that way!

Pat Steinley, for so patiently transforming what we send her into what you are reading. Her willingness to honor the flavor of JC's style, and the rhythm and flow of the way He says things, in deference to "proper" punctuation, is valued greatly;

Katharine Deleot, whose love of the material and willingness to honor her intuition led her to come to us and help proof Volume 2 for publication. The talent and support she so lovingly shares is deeply appreciated and will always be a bond between us;

Karen Gatewood, who is our friend and little sister and who has long been a mirror of our highest Self;

Lili Anne Besson, who nurtures us in so many ways. Currently, she is translating Volume 1 into French;

Our support group (which has expanded to include Dwayne and Cissy Howell, Doris and Melissa Cox, Victor Beasley, Zelma Enloe, Marilyn Spencer, Gloria Markum, LaRae Robinson, and Karen Gatewood) for their on-going and deeply nurturing love;

And to Dee Meek Thompson, Phyllis and Allan Rogers, Brooks Kasson, and Wretha Ingle, for the unconditional way they communicate their love.

Finally, we wish to acknowledge the beautiful souls we were blessed to meet and play with at the Celebration held in Redwood City. The wonderful, joyous flow of support between people from all parts of the country brought fresh meaning to the oneness we all share in consciousness.

INTRODUCTION

Dear Friends,

It isn't possible to relate in words all the changes that have taken place in our life since the publication of Volume 1. The circle of love and support that surrounds us is expanding every day. Even as we reflect now on the experience of sharing our daily guidance, we cannot totally comprehend the extent or magnitude of the changes. So we don't even try anymore. We just accept joy and love and beauty as the natural way to be in the human experience.

We are aware of three major shifts we have made since the original sharing. The first shift is in the total release of obligation and responsibility. JC tells us there really is nothing important about anything in the illusion and we have come to realize that we are not obligated to or responsible for "fixing" anything in the illusion—either for ourself or for anyone else. We are clear that the vital energy that we call Life, is ever-operative and we can choose, each of us, to live in harmony with it or not. The illusion that we create simply gives us the opportunity to choose.

The second shift is recognizing, in expanded ways, the oneness we all are. Actually, it's more than just recognition; it's feeling, in deep and trusting ways, our connectedness with each other. It's a knowing that every person with whom we come in contact is just a facet of our Self, to be unconditionally loved.

The third shift is an acceptance of how easy and simple it all is. Since nothing is important and we have infinite opportunities to choose again, and since there's nothing "out there" but our own Self, what's to be difficult? We are clear that it is truly up to us how easy we will allow it to be.

The most interesting aspect of all this is that the outer details of our life haven't changed that much at all. We still live in the same house on the same busy street, our dogs still teach us in wonderful ways, we still have bills to pay. The difference is in how we feel. It is the feelings of joy and love and peace that are our life now, and we appreciate that the varied activities, such as those described above, are simply the opportunities we give ourself to experience and express these feelings on a more expanded scale.

So where are we today? We still receive our daily meditation, and we still create interesting little challenges for ourself. Yet, there is a knowing that seems to permeate us deeper and deeper every day. It's a knowing that we chose this experience for a purpose; an ever-deepening awareness of that purpose; and a knowing that there's absolutely nothing to keep us from fulfilling that purpose in total joy, if we choose.

As JC would say, "Isn't it a fun game we play?" And how we love playing it with you!

Joyously,

Glenda Lippmann
Grady Claire Porter

Plano, Texas
June, 1985

P. S.—At the end of volume 1, JC indicated it was time for us to study the material and experience the principles he had given us—which, of course, we did. Volume 2 picks up where we left off in Volume 1. Though we received three or four meditations during the summer of our study, it wasn't until the end of August that our guidance began again on a regular basis.

MORNING MEDITATION 7/23/84

Today *is* transformation day!* You are transforming your lives. This is not new to you. It is not a momentous event. It does not portend death, as you call it. Your lives are infinite transformations. You are constantly transforming ideas into action.

I love your path. I love your obedience. And, what is obedience but aligning yourself with principle. Obedience is not some subservient act done to win approval—obedience is knowing the law and knowing your alignment with it. Following your guidance is recognizing the path to alignment. You are on purpose. You are fulfilling your purpose.

You ask about the meditations. I say to you, this is an act of your sharing your Christ. Do not get caught up in the details of doing. Get in touch with the pure joy of sharing your Christ. Get in touch with the excitement of moving out to expand your view of me, for where you send your Christ, you will see the Christ. It is with great joy that I witness your unfolding, for as I have told you, I see you in all your perfection. And yet, I also see you where you think you are. Closer and closer your perception moves to reality. Honor this, little sisters. As you spoke this morning, energize yourself to honoring where you are.

It pleases me that you are seeing how helpful it is to honor where you are, and where are you but with me? Never for an instant are you separated from me, for we are one! Can you be discontent with that?

**We had discovered Ralph Blum's new book,* The Book of Runes, *(St. Martin's Press, New York, 1982). Along with the book comes a set of Runes, which are tiles representing ancient oracles. The Rune Glenda pulled was "Breakthrough or Transformation Day," and Grady pulled "Harvest."*

MORNING MEDITATION 7/30/84

I do not judge you. If you would but realize that viewing yourself without judgment is the simple act of expressing the Christ! You know that I accept you exactly as you are. You are my students remembering your perfection.

There is no purpose in judging. Little sisters, do not judge your judging. You think you have come to a hard part. You see yourself as challenged. You play the game, "Trivial Pursuit,"* and what is that game but remembering what you know. Is it so sad to do? And when you do not remember, are you so bad?

Little sisters, I ask you to focus on me. Release your judgment of yourself. Accept yourself as I accept you. Each time you get caught up in the illusion, look to me. See me accepting you. Do this thing, for in so doing you are fulfilling your purpose. Seeing yourself through my eyes, allowing your Christ to accept you here and now, allows you to accept your Christ here and now.

Feel my love. Truly, there is nothing for you to do but to feel, accept and honor my love.

*"*Trivial Pursuit,*" © *Horn and Abbott, 1983.*

MORNING MEDITATION 8/14/84

I will speak to you, little sisters, about *here and now.*

"Here" is the place of absolute joy, and "now" is the only time there is. You think you move in and out of absolute joy. You perceive yourself on some sort of roller coaster, moving from one emotion to another. I say to you, joy is the only emotion, the only feeling. All the other emotions are merely judgments of joy. As you have just studied, releasing judgment is practicing your perfection. You are never out of the high joy vibration.

You allow events to trigger judgment, thus you experience a perception which you attach to joy and call anger, fear, pain, distrust. Perception is a judgment about what you see. Little ones, you always see perfection, yet you are choosing to judge it and are experiencing the perception of your judgment. Do you see?

You think you must struggle to see perfection. I say to you, the struggle is in your creation—with a little "c"*—of your judgment. Do not judge yourself for this activity. You have seen the process and discussed it, conjuring up all sorts of challenges to the goal in your little game, "Who can be the quietest?"** You do not judge yourself for the funny faces you make, and, you cannot release judgment by condemning yourself for creating it.

The twelve "I AM" Statements*** are absolutely true about you and me, here and now. The process is to become aware of any perception you may have that would negate a statement. Release it, gently, effortlessly, and move back into the absolute joy of total awareness of your "I-Am-ness."

We have talked about being on path. Your perception of this has led you to think you are moving upward to some great spiritual understanding. I say to you, here and now you are perfect. I say to you, here and now you are aware of that perfection. I say to you, your purpose, here and now, is to practice your already existing, total perfection. And, we have already discussed that process.

Here and now I love you! I am with you! I am your Christ expressing, here and now!

**Refers to a concept Arnold Patent uses in his workshop: God "creates" with a capital "C"; our conscious mind creates with a little "c."*

***A game Grady plays with her little nephews when they get noisy in the car. The first one to make a sound loses, so they make funny faces at her, trying to make her giggle so she'll lose the game.*

****See the Be-attitudes at back of book.*

MORNING MEDITATION 8/27/84

It makes no difference through whom I speak. You are never without me.*

I have said, "You cannot put new wine in old bottles." The new wine that you have drunk from my cup does not fit into old belief systems. My wine is pure power, and what you have been experiencing is the power of the new wine shaking the very roots of the old beliefs. You cannot compare your old belief systems with the new, and it is true you can no longer live your life in the old way. The new wine has so infused you that the dissatisfaction you feel, or that is your judgment of it, comes from the surge of new life.

You have not yet known true zest and enthusiasm, for your belief system has attached limited concepts to those qualities. But, dear little ones, the falling away of old beliefs is not death but rich, abundant, joyful, creative, enthusiastic aliveness!

You have been pushed by the power of my wine to new heights of spiritual understanding. You are glimpsing your own perfection. Now, step up higher, here with me. I ask you to stay willing to experience the human condition in a totally new, unfettered, free expression of me. Allow me—allow my truth, my joy, my wisdom, my unconditional love—to express through you here and now.

It is cast off time. It is time to feel the strength of the new wine. It is time to lift your eyes above the belief systems of limitation. It is time to express the unlimited nature of your perfect Self.

We are moving onward and upward together. I ask you to prepare your consciousness. Know your truth! Study the wine. Imbibe it freely so that each moment of your human experience is a full expression of it. You are on path, little sisters. Honor that. You have not strayed one jot or one tittle. As the small sprout shoots upward through the crusty earth, so you burst forward in the freedom, in the light of the fullness of universal harmony.

Dear little Glenda, let not your heart be troubled. I have said to you, "View me. Expand your view of me." Do not allow it to be filtered by beliefs of judgment. And you are doing this! Feel my love! Feel my joy! Feel my enthusiasm! Take it as yours! It is ever here, ever flowing in abundance, coursing through you. Little sisters, feel my trust! I know who I am, thus, as you partake of me, you know your "I AM."

As you wipe away the tears of yesterday, your smile is here and now. There is no effort—merely a dab, and the tears are gone. I cannot forsake you, for it is in you I live and move and have my being. Celebrate!

**We were trying to decide who the meditation would come through this morning when JC began speaking through Grady.*

MORNING MEDITATION 8/29/84

You speak of omnipresence.* Do you see me? I am with you at all times, under every circumstance—my love, my joy. You are surrounded by my infinite embrace.

Little ones, do not trouble yourself with the details of illusion. I ask you to focus on me—more than just a simple awareness of my presence. I ask you to focus on feeling me active within you. Time is not a limitation, except in your belief system. How much time do you give me? I ask you to allow me to flow through you, all ways and always.

Releasing the perception of importance, of duty, of obligation—these are ways to honor me. You are not responsible to me; you do not have a duty to me. There is no obligation owed me. It is only through your free choice, your opening up willingly and joyfully, that I flow through you. Of course, we are one, yet your perception at this time clouds your view of our oneness. It is this cloud you are ready to release, this perception of your obligation to the illusion. You wonder, "What will I do if I do not meet my obligations?" Release that, for you know your awareness is expanding to include the knowledge that *I do through you.* Do you think I will leave you stranded? No. No, you are becoming aware of the power of my truth. And, you are ready to utilize this truth here and now, ready to know this truth so absolutely that confusion, deliberation, consternation, are replaced automatically in your consciousness by my truth.

If someone says to you, "2 + 2 = ?" the truth of "4" immediately comes to your consciousness. Likewise, if someone says to you, "2 + 2 = 5," the truth of "4" comes to your consciousness to deny the "5," not to be angry with it, merely to replace it. I wish my truth to flow through you in that way.

I have said, "Know the truth, and it will make you free." From what? Untruth! False belief is your only burden. Your willingness, your loving willingness, has brought you to this point of release of any burden, any impairment of your vision, any cloudy mist that would distort the reality of what we are.

Now, feel my joy in you. Feel that warm pleasantness in the center of your being, flowing out of each pore. It is a light that surrounds you, pouring forth from inside, out. I am in the high joy vibration in you.

**Our friend, Karen, had spent the night and was preparing to meditate with us when she jokingly teased Grady about being omnipresent.*

MORNING MEDITATION 8/31/84

You are full of nothing but love. Your perception of the situations in your life need not be dirty and smelly.* You have but to choose absolute joy.

Let us look at the process of releasing false beliefs. I have said to you, "Everything is perfect." That which would seem to interrupt your clear, expanded view of me is not there to be judged, to be understood, to be analyzed, or even to be figured out. Dear little ones, it is an illusion. It is an error, an error like "2 + 2 = 5." It is also what you came here to see through.

I have said to you, "All is perfect." And, we know the absolute truth of that statement. Perfection expressed is the activity of God. It is the heartbeat of the universe. Perfection expressed is the livingness you chose in this human experience. Open yourself to the joy of seeing through your illusion. You play your little games, challenging yourself to remember this fact or that fact. You get together with friends, and you play on the field, exercising what you know. You are choosing to play. And, I say to you, That is your choice for coming to this human experience—to play! You do not look at "Trivial Pursuit"** as some tragedy in your life that is taxing the very limits of your experience. You do not look at the game upon the field as some accident that you happen to be involved in.

I have said to you, "False belief is your only burden." And, my little children, the only false belief is that you could be separate from me, that just maybe there is some condition, some circumstance, some person, that through some force, could wrench you away from my love. The game you choose to play here and now is to practice, to exercise, that this cannot be so. It is not a game you win or lose. It is a game you enjoy. You affirm that nothing can separate you from the infinite love of the Christ. Now, play the game of practicing that. The illusion that would challenge is your playmate and allows you the challenging experience of using what you know to enjoy the game. It is saying to you, "I bet you I can make you believe you can be separated." Now, is that an enemy? Do you see? *You can love it all!*

Arnold has told you, and so have I, that joy is all there is. Get in touch with your joy. Love the game. Excite yourself with each opportunity. When you busy yourself with false belief, you cloud your view of me. Releasing those clouds, pushing them aside, is such fun! You already know what you will see. The joy comes in the releasing—the great game of *release.*

Honor your willingness. Honor the enthusiasm you are already aware of. Focus on that.

**One of the dogs had diarrhea during the night and much of the morning had been spent cleaning the carpet.*

MORNING MEDITATION 9/1/84

How I love you, my little ones!

You ask about *perfection*. I see you as perfect. And, what do I see? I see love, life, truth, health, joy, abundance. I see spirit operating as soul, operating in principle.

Perfection is principle in action. Perfection is the infinite activity of God. As such, I could never speak to you all there is about perfection. For you, here and now, claiming your perfection, I say to you, view yourself as one who moves forward in love. You are attempting to squeeze your flesh and bone identity into a concept that gives you form and definition. It is a trick you play on yourself. It is like you ask your conscious mind to conjure up an image of infinity. You attempt to see vast spaces moving out farther and farther, saying to yourself, "Surely somewhere out there—beyond my ability to conceive—there is an end." I say to you, as I said to you before, "You cannot place this new thinking into old, limited beliefs." You cannot ask to understand perfection—to put it into the framework of limited beliefs held in your conscious mind.

You are here and now perfect. I have given you ways to see this perfection. I have said to you, "Step up higher." And, when you do this thing in your consciousness, the desire to understand is meaningless . . . and released. You do not need to understand a sunset to enjoy its beauty. The "I AM" Statements* lift your consciousness here with me. You say, "I don't always believe that." It is the truth. And, applying the truth brings about the result of truth, whether you believe it or not. If you use the principle "2 + 2 = 4," you do not have to believe the principle, but the result is the same. Use of the principle consistently, supports your belief system. You are doing this thing. In each experience you are applying the principles. Yet, you are still running back down in your consciousness to see if it worked.

Principle always results in principle. When I spoke to you about outcomes, that is what I meant. As you turn to me each day, as you commit to exercising and practicing your perfection, you bring yourself to the higher view. It is not an elevator going up and down. You are perfect. You do not need to understand perfection. The principles we have shared, exercised, trusted and loved are the answer you seek now. I am here by your side, inside, acting through you. I know perfection. I trust perfection. I am perfection.

Allow me to be your own perfection.

**See Be-attitudes at the back of this book.*

MORNING MEDITATION 9/2/84

You are releasing the illusion.* Honor this thing. You wish me to put my arm around you and comfort you. I always love you, but, little ones, there is nothing to comfort. I see perfection in all things. I see you seeing perfection. Release the belief that you are experiencing something other than perfection.

It is with great love that I see you opening your consciousness—accepting, feeling, enjoying your perfection. You are remembering that work is done in consciousness. Releasing is done in consciousness.

Do not attach yourself to the illusion. Do not buy into the illusion of "loss." The evidence presented you by the illusion is your opportunity to express joyful abundance, vital health, awareness of the ever-presence and infinity of life. Recognizing the totality of life, experiencing the awareness of Infinite Presence is joyful and is the fulfilling of your purpose. You are releasing the illusion of limited concepts. Honor this, little sisters, honor this thing. Nothing is going on with your precious ones but joyful freedom, exuberant life. And, they serve their purpose in allowing you to see through the limited illusion to the true reality.

I love your willingness, your turning to me, lifting your consciousness, allowing me to express through you here and now. There is nothing to fear. All is well.

**When we awoke this morning, Dawn, our beloved Weimaraner of 12 years, could not stand up. We recognized that she was bringing us an illusion to be released. Seeing her as perfect, and being willing to totally release any false belief we held that clouded our view of her perfection, we lovingly tended her. She is still with us, bringing us new lessons all the time.*

MORNING MEDITATION 9/7/84

How lovingly, willingly, you follow me. Here in the high joy vibration, our arms linked in love, we practice our perfection together.

I love your honoring what we have shared. Choosing me above all else is not the end, but the beginning. As the false perceptions fall away, your view and expression of me—the pure Christ consciousness—opens you to joy, abundance, and aliveness beyond which your limited concepts now can behold.

Cleaning and clearing the windows of your inner self allows you to look in and see your perfection. It is from this perfection that you look out and see the beauty, see the love, see the vitality of God's infinite universe. Seeing, in this sense, is total experience. Beholding is becoming. It is true, you are totally perfect here and now. We are speaking of releasing limited perceptions to the actual awareness and experience of your perfection. Honor your choice. Recognize the love you express for me in committing to your study. Appreciate your faithfulness. It is your strength, little sisters. It is the light that expands your spiritual awareness.

Go forward now in the highest sense of joy and enthusiasm toward this activity you have chosen. Nothing—absolutely nothing — can stop you now. Let's go!

MORNING MEDITATION 9/12/84

It is I who speak through you in these choices. It is your Christ consciousness that is aware of your ideal day.* I am in, through, and acting as you. Honor this. Little sisters, honor that you are releasing those perceptions that in the past you believed separated us. Honor that it is your Christ that practices Its perfection. It is not Grady and Glenda "trying" to do these things. It is your Christ that is aware of, performing, enjoying, and living your perfection, here and now. See this thing. See that I am expressing through you here and now.

**The meditation today came after we had done our Ideal Day Exercise (learned in Arnold Patent's Workshop). JC was reminding us it is our Christ consciousness that chooses the ingredients for our perfect day. This is what we chose to experience:*

IDEAL DAY 9/12/84 *We are unlocking ourself from any false belief that we perceive would close us in, or in any way limit the full, free flow of abundance in and out of our experience. We are releasing any attachment to misperceptions about ourself or those precious ones in our care.*

We are gleeful in our activities and are fully aware of, and focusing on, the absolute perfection of our life. We are 100% committed to expressing our perfection in every facet of our experience. We are enjoying the highest sense of home, of productive activity, of companionship, of abundance, of health, of peace and unconditional love. We honor our willingness and our growth.

In acknowledging the perfection in our life, we are releasing any belief of time limitations, space limitations, money limitations or peaceful surrounding limitations. We honor our total alignment with the universe and its divine order, releasing any outcome, and enjoying zestful and enthusiastic awareness of our alignment.

We totally trust and believe the absolute truth of all of the above.

MORNING MEDITATION 9/14/84

I AM. Little sisters, you are knowing *I AM.* I ask you to identify with the "I." It is our oneness. Your openness to your identity, to your I Am-ness, is the activity of God in you. This openness allows the full, free flow of perfection in and through you. You are not separate from this perfection. You are not a stationary object through which perfection flows. You are in it and of it. You are seeing this thing. You are moving beyond your conscious mind references. You are allowing the belief systems that you perceived separated you to dissolve into their native nothingness. This process, which you are now observing, without judgment, is the final release. Moving into infinite perfection is the expanding, beyond your belief systems, of your view of the Christ. As always, this is a shift in consciousness.

You are wondering how this changes your human experience. What difference does it make? Operating in and as perfection eliminates in your own thinking the need for the experience to be one way or the other. Absolute joy is the activity of perfection.

I have said to you, "Little sisters, we are one—that through you I live and act." It is time for you to trust this thing. It is time for you to be so filled with this Christ consciousness that you own and honor it truly is I that is your "I."

I AM. From this moment forward, claim me as your *I AM.* You no longer need wonder what JC would do. I am doing through you, being through you, loving, living, practicing my perfection as you. You are ready. Like your game, "Ready or Not" . . . here I am. This is not a burden. This is not an obligation. This is not something you will "try" to live up to. It is . . . now.

I AM. I am you, and "you am I."

MORNING MEDITATION 9/17/84

It is here in the high joy vibration that the Christ in you unites with the Christ in me. You are open and willing, for I am open and willing. It is I who acts and loves in and through you. Behold your Christ. Express your Christ. Manifest the Christ consciousness.

In releasing false beliefs you are moving (or so you think of movement) into the awareness of the allness—the allness of love, the allness of life, the allness of abundance. Releasing the belief systems that cloud your view of allness is the step you are taking now. You have said that stepping out in consciousness without belief systems is as if stepping into a void. I ask you to step up higher. You need not understand allness to experience it. You are ready to release your need to understand. The shift is to experiencing. Our little brother, Arnold,* has told you that it is a feeling experience. He is clear on this thing.

In the experience level is absolute trust; the flow of allness is what permeates your consciousness. It is the release of details. Experience your Christ. Feel the love, not as some outside energy, but rather as your own. See it as your playmate. Claim it. Honor it.

**Arnold Patent, who is in our meditation group today.*

MORNING MEDITATION 9/18/84

You are indeed on purpose. Little sisters, you create your challenges to practice your perfection. I see you as perfect. If, in my name, you choose to challenge yourself, recognize your Christ consciousness playfully moving you to a place of joy.

Your belief systems that would say there is a power beyond you, to correct you, to condemn you, to punish you, are just that—false beliefs you are ready to release. And how do you release a false belief? In your consciousness. Remind yourself—and you are doing this thing with your self-made challenges—that there is nothing to do to be on purpose. Learning to open yourself to the joyful abundance of the universe is the step you are taking. You do not decide how this is manifest in your human experience. You need not decide, for you cannot even see all the abundant ways your experience is enriched. The process of opening yourself to your abundance is releasing thoughts about how you must receive it or thoughts about how you must act (or not act) in the process.

Our little brother, Arnold,* has told you, "Be clear." Being clear is being without conscious mind. It is clearing your channel of false beliefs so that infinite intelligence is pouring into you, guiding you. We spoke of allness, experiencing allness. I say to you, be clear. Open yourself totally, and then flow with the energy that comes through. You need decide nothing. As you allow the Christ consciousness to operate in you, it is done. You merely sit back and enjoy. Whatever energy need be expressed, whatever love, whatever support is called for in your environment will be provided through you—automatically.

Let us speak of *being clear.*

This is the process of releasing beliefs about yourself that you create to confuse you. You think some beliefs were created a long time ago and keep coming into your experience. I say to you, here and now, you are clear. If there is in your perception a false belief to cloud your view, you have created it here and now. So what? Un-create it! Stop thinking about it, and move back into that full, free flow of light and intelligence of your Christ consciousness. Little sisters, you are on path, and you are playing with yourself and each other with your little creations. It is the process of practicing your perfection. Enjoy your perfection. Enjoy when you challenge yourself. I say to you, honor your perfection. Honor your awareness of your perfection.

**Another reference to our friend, Arnold Patent.*

MORNING MEDITATION 9/19/84

Let us speak of *letting go.*

It is true that you look very carefully at what you are holding onto and try to understand the substance of what you might move to. Little sisters, you cannot know in your conscious mind, for it is the conscious mind you are releasing. It is that need to know that you are releasing. You do not feel secure in conscious mind, and yet you feel reluctant to release the "security" of conscious mind. The conscious mind makes no sense. So what? You are releasing the need to have things "make sense."

You do not yet choose to honor it, but the old bottles have broken open.* You feel you have no place to put your new wine. I say to you, you cannot contain the new wine. You cannot place it in limited concepts. It flows so abundantly that the whole universe cannot contain it. It is your openness through which the wine flows. You do not direct it—it directs you. Open your hands . . . you are holding onto nothingness. See your hands open. Feel the abundance flowing in through your fingers, permeating yourself and flowing back out again. You have no lack of trust. Your perception is aware, here and now, of your perfection. Honor this and free yourself forever of the need to understand.

You are playful ones, and you will continue to create for yourself little challenges—as a child creates a castle in the sand. The child sits and plays in his mind in the castle, enjoys his visions, and then allows the flow to move in and wash away the whole illusion. "So what?" he says. And, when he chooses to play again, he builds another castle, for the sand is infinite, and the joy is infinite. Releasing your identity as something more than just a playful child is where you choose to struggle. You are attaching some importance to purpose, some importance that the universe needs you to decide your purpose so that you can contribute to its harmonious working. That's not what your little brother said to you. You are on purpose, because you *are*. You're not "becoming." You're not "gonna be." You *are*.

It's okay to stay in conscious mind and create your games. Recognize that it is nothing more than your perfect Self "playing like." "Play like I'm this, play like you're that." The purpose of play is joy. You are on purpose. I ask you to honor that. Do you know what I mean by "honor?" Honor is total awareness, appreciation, love, unconditional support, acceptance. So, I say to you, honor your perfection. You can, here and now, choose to honor.

**See MORNING MEDITATION 8/27/84.*

MORNING MEDITATION 9/21/84

Releasing judgment about the illusion is releasing perception about the way things should or should not be. Allowing each creature, each soul, the opportunity to express—each in its own individual way—is releasing judgment.

Little sisters, illusion truly is a game. Release the rules of the game. You find yourself so busy directing the play of the game that you do not enjoy it. Now, that is your perception of yourself. Your Christ-Self is in full awareness and is giving you the full opportunity to express in any way you choose. Your chosen purpose is to expand your view of your Christ-Self.

You are not in the business of changing anything—not the illusion, not yourself. Your purpose in expanding your view of joy is exactly as the word implies. You're not changing your view, you're expanding—releasing limitation—so that your awareness of joy is experienced at higher and higher levels. Do not attach judgment to change, and since "expand" to you does not carry that judgment, stay with that.

The temptation to "understand" is at release point. You are truly aware of your divine identity. Everything else that you perceive is your creation. Using the illusion to express your divine identity is an activity of joy. And, since it is your creation, let it be majestic to you. Let it be magnificent to you. Let it be elegant . . . triumphant! It is expanding your view from mediocre to majestic that is your joyful exercise. You are clear on this thing. Your perception of yourself as reluctant, doubtful, resistant children is just the role you created to step into and express your divine identity.

The curtain is up!

MORNING MEDITATION 9/24/84

Ah, little sisters, the beauty of it all! You are on purpose. You feel on purpose. You are tasting the joy of your purpose.

You ask me of *sharing.*

I have told you, "There are infinite ways in which to share your beheld Christ." Opening yourself to the Christ in all you see, in all you hear, in all you touch, is your purpose. I say to you, acting in purpose is the activity of God. Stay open to allow that activity to express in and through you.

There is no one way to do this thing, and you do not decide. The purpose of the Christ is to reveal Itself to you. Your purpose is to expand your view of this revelation. Open yourself as a "view-er" and not a "do-er." Observe my unfolding infinity. That it is done through you is evidence of your willingness to allow me to express myself through you. You know you are not a casual observer but are committed to seeing this Christ as operative in all things. Ah! And, you are doing this thing.

As you move forward to share, stay on purpose. Expand your view in this activity. Do not be tempted to feel that you have something someone else does not. Your purpose is to see it there. Sharing what I say with you is helpful when shared from strength and purpose. Your Christ reaching out to touch the beheld Christ in others serves your purpose.

I have touched the one you call Victor, and he knows it. See his Christ so that he may see it. I care not how you share or with whom you share. Your purpose—to expand your view of me—is all I ask of you.

Stay clear. Stay open. And, I will create for you in your

awareness beautiful music, melodious teaching, joyful experiencing. You view. I do.

I treasure the music you bring me in your openness.

And, to the one you call Frances, see the Christ. There is no loss in me. Say to her that all is well. That which she has nurtured is active and purposeful. Love surrounds her.*

**A message to a dear friend whose son left the human experience unexpectedly.*

MORNING MEDITATION 9/25/84

"And the truth shall set you free."

What is the *truth?*

I am the truth—the truth about you. The Christ is the reality of the relationship you have with God. It is a simple truth. Love is truth, the perfect interaction between God and man. "Man" is the term used here to identify the soul that is expressing God's activity. It is the term used for the awareness of God. Your identity is the awareness of God. The term is certainly limited. The awareness of God is unlimited, but since we are still using words to communicate with each other, it will serve.

You think of truth as a fact, or perhaps a statement without error. Truth is an active power that is your life energy. You express truth when you allow this active, vital energy to flow in, through, and as you without conscious mind interruption. You don't "tell" the truth; you "are" the truth. You need not concern yourself with the illusion when truth is your activity. You may yet observe the illusion but, as truth, you are aware of, but in no way influenced by, the illusion. It truly is a "So what?" situation. As truth, you are totally aware that the illusion is for your entertainment and joy.

Staying in truth, staying open to the uninterrupted flow of this energy, allows you to look at the illusion without judgment. This is the majesty about which we spoke earlier. Judging the illusion as bad or good, poor or rich is the conscious mind's attempt to have you believe you can be separated from truth. You do not need to look for truth. You do not need to figure out what truth is. Open yourself—without judgment—and you behold, you feel, you are aware of the activating power of truth. It does not come and go. It is your life—your infinite life. And, indeed it frees you from your false beliefs based on judgment.

Open yourself now to your truth. View your truth operating in and as you. Be delighted with it. Allow yourself to be transformed by it. Because, truly releasing the judgments about yourself and any false beliefs about your identity, freeing yourself by allowing truth to flow in you, as you, transforms everything in your life. For now, through this releasing, you are only aware of truth . . . me . . . the Christ . . . unconditional love . . . peace . . . exquisite joy.

How's that for an ideal day?! And, little sisters, it's yours. It's mine. It's ours!*

**We are struck by the infinite beauty of the Christ expressing to us. We own it as our heritage. We were not chosen; we chose. We are moving forward in the absolute truth of our identity. It's knowing. It's like Prince Charles knows he's of royal birth, and he would never accept anything less than royal treatment, because he knows he deserves it. Well, we are truth. That is our divine identity. It is our inheritance, because we are mothered and fathered by truth and love.* — G & GC.

MORNING MEDITATION 9/28/84

Coming together, in love, is truly the high joy vibration.* The joining of your Christ-Self is the experience of the high joy vibration.

You need not trouble yourself with conscious mind judgments about this joy. You are opening yourself to the experience of the high joy vibration. You are freeing yourself from the limitations of the conscious mind. Honor this. Put energy into honoring this thing. The experiences of your day are taking on new dimensions. You are aware of this and, yet, there still is the temptation to fit it into conscious mind acceptance. It is helpful for you to release the need to understand.

The freedom about which you speak is found in consciousness. The activities that you imagine do not bring you that freedom. Freedom—beheld in consciousness—brings you these activities and many, many more.

When I speak to you of *consciousness,* it is beyond the conscious mind. Consciousness is your full awareness of your Christ-Self, your beauty, your joy, your wealth, your unconditional love. And, when you act in consciousness, that is your environment.

The joy that I experience, the love I feel at your laughter, the companionship of your presence with me in your own togetherness, is my own awareness of my Christ-Self expressing through you. I have said to you, "My purpose is to reveal myself to you, and yours is to see more and more of me." We are on purpose. You are feeling the joy of this purpose. You are experiencing the exquisite sweetness of our togetherness. I honor this. I ask you to honor this thing with me.

**In Austin with Brooks, Karen, Glenda and GC.*

MORNING MEDITATION 9/29/84

Ah, little sisters, the joy of our togetherness!*

Releasing your conscious mind beliefs is the process of opening yourself to me. You are doing this thing, here and now. Ask yourself, "Do you feel my presence?" Release anything in your conscious mind that you perceive would separate us, here and now. Take a moment, and feel my presence. Pause to get in touch with the feeling. Do this thing for yourself daily.

Releasing the conscious mind beliefs is expressing your Christ. You speak of "channels." *You are my channels.* I have told you, "It is through you—each of you—that I live, and move, and have my being." You are my be-ingness.

You have asked me of things you have read about me.** Everything said or written about me is the perception of the writer or speaker. It is here and now I speak to you directly. You need not Grady Claire.*** Open yourself to your Christ. I have said to the one, Grady Claire and Glenda, "You have walked the path of coming to me," and now you others are doing this thing. I say to each of you, I am alive, joyful, loving, active and speaking to you. Open yourself to me. That means, release the judgment that says you cannot hear me. When you laugh, you laugh with me. When you feel joy, you are feeling my joy. And, when you love, it is the pure Christ love expressing through you. That is what I mean, little sisters, by "you are doing this thing."

Do not judge yourself. It is not helpful. And, I remind you of the clouds. Judgment has no power. Like clouds, it is merely a mist to distort the perfection you look upon. You may choose to look upon it, or you may effortlessly and joyously move the clouds away.

This is not serious; it is not important; it is not heavy. Those are the things in your belief system you are ready to release. Feel the joy. That's all! Feel the joy.

I wish to speak to you later on *responsibility.*

Feel my love now. Move forward in this day, in love. We will speak soon.

**In Austin, at Lili's, with Karen, Lili, Glenda and GC.*

***There was a question about something written in the Bible that indicated Jesus was angry.*

****Today's message was coming through GC.*

MORNING MEDITATION 9/30/84

The beauty of it all!* Little ones, you are sensing the high joy vibration. You are experiencing in sound, in sight, in feel, in awareness, the beauty of God. Recognize your consciousness creates this for you. Recognize that it is your awareness of beauty that allows you to experience it. You may see this beauty anywhere if you open your awareness to it.

Let us speak now of *responsibility.*

You have played with this word many times. You have a judgment attached to the word so that obligation and debt are synonymous. You have played with the word in terms of your ability to respond.** I say to you, the word has no meaning. It is a word attached to conscious mind. It is the judgment that links you to detail. You have no responsibility—not to me, not to anything. The ego investment in that word ties you to a limited consciousness, and you are ready to be free of this limited perception.

You are the expression of God. You do not have a responsibility to express. In reality, you have no choice to express. The only choice you have about your be-ingness is to be aware of it. That choice—to be aware—is not a responsibility.

You are the expression of love. That is your essence. It is not separated from your experience here and now, unless you choose to separate yourself from it in awareness.

So, you may release the word "responsibility" from your consciousness. I see that you are becoming aware of how our communication is beginning to evolve. You are dropping this word and you are dropping that word.*** Do you see? As you open yourself, as you free your consciousness from judgment, you are releasing judgmental terms so that communication is transferring to another level. Awareness of feelings, without attaching judgment thereto, is the communication I speak of. I have said to you, "Feel my love." And, you have. I have said to you, "Feel my presence." And, you have. (I "feel" the speed.)**** It is in this way we are beginning to communicate. There is no judgment in these feelings—only awareness.

So, feel your day! Feel the love, the beauty, as you are doing here and now. Honor that you are communicating with your God-Self. Little sisters, *there is nothing else.*

**Glenda had suggested we go to City Park this morning before breakfast. It is an old, beautiful park and camping area located on the banks of Lake Austin. The area was virtually deserted. The water was clear and sparkled in the sun, and the crispness of the autumn morning was so fresh and invigorating that each breath was a celebration. We honored the feelings and had our meditation in this setting.*

***Not feeling comfortable with the usual connotation of the term, we had long viewed it as "response-ability."*

****A reference to the deleting of words or phrases belonging to conscious mind activities such as "think," "figure out," "understand," etc.*

*****JC, through Grady, was talking rapidly, and Glenda, who was transcribing, was having to race to get it all down. He sensed the speed needed to keep up and lovingly acknowledged it. He also slowed down.*

MORNING MEDITATION 10/1/84

Yes, little sisters, you are ready. You are ready to release your judgment about your identity. The conscious mind picture that you think you have painted yourself into is a caricature of your true Self. Look at the picture lovingly, laughingly, ah, non-judgmentally, and the picture will show you the limited beliefs about yourself that you are ready to release!

Each of you, in your own way, has opened yourself to me. Even in the illusion you cannot now close the door, and in the opening comes the opportunity to expand. Expand your awareness of your true identity—me, the Christ! You do not go looking for the Christ. *You open yourself to your Self.* Removing the false beliefs that you have chosen to create is expanding your view of the Christ.

Your conscious mind still would like to complicate it, because that is one of the purposes you have given the conscious mind. Be open. Release the false belief that there is something you can lose by being open to releasing responsibility. Stay in consciousness in this thing. Do nothing. *Do nothing!* No thing. Stay in consciousness!

Feel my love. Feel my presence. Feel my beauty like the wind upon your face. When I say to you, "There is nothing else," what I say to you is, who *wants* anything else?

MORNING MEDITATION 10/2/84

This truly is work done in consciousness.* Your image, Grady Claire, of the three of us sitting cross-legged, knees touching, holding hands in the middle of the bank,** releasing the fear, is the process of working in consciousness.

Placing yourself in a perceived frightening situation, allowing yourself to experience the old fears or judgments, then detaching the judgment from the feeling, allows you to see that the circumstances are not the cause of the fear. Doing this, in consciousness, allows you the additional feelings of my presence. It is the process of using me to clear yourself so that I may use you.

You are on path! I have said to you, I say to you now, *honor it.* To honor is to strengthen your awareness. Take time now, again, to sit with me and honor your willingness. I ask you not to focus on what you have not done but just to honor that you feel my presence.

So, feel my love. Feel my joy. Feel my presence as we sit together . . . and, feel it appreciatingly.

**We had studied the 4/30/84 MEDITATION before starting today's meditation.*

*** The bank where we do business.*

MORNING MEDITATION 10/4/84

Do you know what the birds would do with money?

They would shred it and weave it amongst the twigs and branches of their nests.* You are on purpose, little sisters, opening yourself to the Christ consciousness, releasing the judgments that you perceive would block your view. I wish to remind you that you have a full, free view of me and that you are creating the illusion to practice your perfection.

You are abundance. Your very essence is abundance—abundant love, abundant joy, abundant aliveness, beauty, light. Do not forget that you create these illusions to exercise that abundance. The outcome expected in the illusion is of no purpose. For example, in your arithmetic book are many different problems—exercises to give you the opportunity to practice certain principles—multiplication, division, addition and subtraction. Now, the answers are in the back of the book. And, if you choose, you can go there and get all the right answers. But, that is not the purpose of the problems in the book. They are there to give you the joyful activity of using what you know.

When you are focused on exercising what you know, the answer makes no difference, because you feel in touch with the principle. As you go through and do your long division, it is the feeling that comes in the process that is the purpose of the exercise.

I have said, "Your purpose is to expand your view of me." There is no outcome in that exercise! It is the feeling—the joy, the trust, the certainty—that comes in the process of expanding. For truly, I am all you see.

I have said to you that I honor you. Do not deceive yourself that you want more approval than that. *I honor you.*

**We had been exploring the concept of money.*

MORNING MEDITATION 10/8/84

(Grady Claire)

I have spoken to you as JC so that you could become aware of our oneness with the Christ. Indeed, I now speak as you. And, it is our challenge to allow the Christ consciousness to exercise Itself.

Accepting your identity is staying in the high joy vibration.

We are doing this thing.

(Glenda)

You are my followers. I lead you to new heights, new vistas. I thrust you into spacelessness and timelessness, so that you may roam the heavens and see our oneness.

I give you everything. You need nothing.

MORNING MEDITATION 10/11/84

Feel my presence . . . .

That which speaks to us is the Christ and does not come only in meditation. We can trust everything as perfect if we release conscious mind judgment of it.

Let us start our day affirming our Christ-Self—being clear about who we are—then moving out in joy, in enthusiasm and in absolute trust to play the game presented by the events in our lives, the events as they come. Releasing the need to orchestrate these events opens us to the spontaneity that we just felt.*

Having the opportunity to go here or there is like landing on a particular spot in the game board.** You may choose to purchase — or follow the directions on that particular spot—or not. It's just part of the game. Staying out of conscious mind means staying out of reasoning why you should or should not do this thing. How does it feel?

Honor us. Be aware, accepting, and acknowledging of our Christ-Self.

**Our friend, Eddie, had called just prior to the meditation and, out of the blue, urged us to go to London with him in a couple of days.*

***A reference to our previous discussions on money. We had used the analogy of the game Monopoly to get in touch with how freeing it was to play with money with a sense of abandonment and the realization it didn't matter, because "it was just a game."*

MORNING MEDITATION 10/12/84

Come up here to the high place. Open yourself to me. Open yourself to the Christ—the Christ in you. Honor your Christ-Self and act accordingly.

You play the games of conscious mind, and yet I have said to you, "I am acting in you—I am moving in you—I am having my being as you." Only the conscious mind is afraid to act. Only the conscious mind judges this or judges that. There is no fear in me. There is no lack in me. Acting in love, reaching out in love, is expanding your view of the Christ. Only the conscious mind sees reasons why and why not.

Free yourself, little sisters, from the conscious mind! It is in consciousness where we meet. It is in consciousness where your work is done. And, it *is* done. There is nothing for you to do. Reaching out in love is not "doing" — it is expressing your Christ.

Stay in consciousness. Move forward in love. Be clear. Be clear. Only the conscious mind wants to protect. Only the conscious mind fears loss. Reaching out in unconditional love is expanding your view of the Christ.

MORNING MEDITATION 10/17/84

Yes, come to the high place with me. Feel my presence. Claim your identity, but do not let conscious mind outline the details of this identity. You play with the conscious mind idea that the Christ would not do this, or the Christ should not do that. Dear ones, the Christ *is*, and the illusion about you does not describe the Christ.

You say to yourself now you feel discomfort, out of alignment, sick. I say to you, as I have already said to you through your soul partner, Glenda, joy is all there is!* Judging your feelings, calling them this or that, is what you're ready to release—the judgment.

Do not shy away from this activity. Do not judge yourself as bad because the opportunity is in your path. Do not struggle and pain yourself. *Release the judgment.*

I have said to you, "You may do this in the twinkling of an eye," but if you do not do it in the twinkling of an eye, it's okay. Do not judge yourself about your judgment.

Your little brother, Arnold, has told you that you want what you have in your experience. I support that at one level. Your consciousness is only aware of me. Your conscious mind is the activity of your beliefs and judgments. Bringing the conscious mind in alignment with consciousness truly gives you the freedom to function in the human experience in perfect joy and perfect trust. This means you could sit in the midst of what conscious mind might previously have described as squalor, pestilence and pain, that you could, indeed, sit there in absolute joy and trust. But, what I say to you is, the alignment of conscious mind and consciousness sees *only* joy—sees *only* perfection.

Release trying to "figure out," and follow me. The path I

have laid out for you is simple. You cannot judge and expand your view of me. I say to you, you are doing this thing. You are releasing judgment. You are feeling my presence. I say to you now, act as the Christ.

**This morning when I was feeling sick at my stomach, Glenda had said, "Release it; there's nothing but joy in there anyway. Let the joy come out."*

MORNING MEDITATION 10/21/84

(We read MORNING MEDITATION 4/8/84 prior to this meditation).

You are doing this thing—you are recognizing when the conscious mind suggests you are not doing this thing.

I wish to say to you that you are in alignment. At this point, you see yourself experiencing the results of conscious mind. I ask you to move to the other side. Conscious mind cannot act without your energy. It cannot move to create anything without your permission. Conscious mind does not have a mind of its own.

Establishing awareness of alignment is placing your energy and focus on the total awareness of consciousness. Without the focus of this energy, conscious mind uses the energy to create for you the illusions of your belief system. You have a saying: "Not to decide is a decision." The same is true here. Not to focus in consciousness is the permission conscious mind needs to create. It's okay to allow conscious mind to create your challenges, just like it's okay to sit down and play a game. But, what I say to you is, you have the choice. If you are choosing to stay focused in consciousness, conscious mind can create nothing. This is the power of the Christ.

Focusing in consciousness is the high joy vibration.

MORNING MEDITATION 10/22/84

Dear little sisters, you have the truth before you. Where is your joy? Choosing the high joy vibration, choosing to focus yourself in consciousness, is what you are challenging yourself to do.

The "doing" of conscious mind does not fulfill you. "Doing nothing," when judged by conscious mind, does not fulfill you. Choosing consciousness, choosing to be aware of, in touch with, loving, trusting, enjoying the awareness of the Christ, is the step you are taking.

I have said to you, "Feel my presence." It is the key to the perfect joyous experience you wish to have. Feel my presence. It is not hard to do. It does not tire you out. There is no effort. Feel . . . my . . . presence ....

I have shown you the exquisiteness of absolute joy. When you watched the baby goats, jumping for the sheer joy of jumping, spontaneously responding to the joyous energy within them, that is the joy of my presence. Feel that joy. Feel the love that will bring you that joy. There is nothing else. No matter how creatively the conscious mind paints the illusion, joy — and the full, free expression of it—is all there is.

Choose to believe this. Choose to align yourself with this, for indeed it is in this thing you are fulfilled—and so is your purpose.

MORNING MEDITATION 10/23/84

You are on purpose. I ask you now to choose me, to identify with me, as me. Open yourself to me. This means, give me access in, through, and as you. Conscious mind resists this by your permission. Focusing on allowing me, the Christ consciousness, to live, move and have beingness as you, denies the conscious mind permission or power.

I have said to you, "I see you in total perfection." That is because I see myself in you. Little sisters, I ask you only to see the same.

The new Be-attitudes* are our affirmation of oneness. Take me with you as you move from this quiet place. Take me with you. Take me to your office. Ride with me on the roads. Wherever you go, take me. This is the taking that prospers not only you and me, but all who touch your life.**

Allow me to be, in you. Be me.

**Another reference to the "I AM" Statements located in the back of the book.*

***This was a reference to some study we had done on the word "taking," wherein we realized that releasing all the negative judgment and connotations surrounding that word indeed opened us up to receive our good.*

MORNING MEDITATION 10/24/84

Hello, *joy!* Hello, *beauty!* Hello, *abundance, exuberance!*

Greet your good! Acknowledge its presence in your life. Open the door to the beautiful, the abundant, the vitality that you perceive to be outside yourself. Open your arms in glorious welcome to these beloved friends. Dear ones, as you do this thing, as you practice your openness, what fills your arms in joyous embrace but your own awareness of your own true Self.

It is true that you can take the conscious mind's path to awareness—the step-by-step process of going from not knowing to knowing. And that's okay. I offer you the path of total knowing . . . now. It is simple. Release the judgments and beliefs of conscious mind.

The drama of the illusion is creatively produced by the conscious mind to entangle you emotionally in its fantasy. It is a game you choose to play and extricate yourself from ever so carefully back to the knowing that it is a game. Choosing knowing is choosing me, and choosing me allows us to expand our awareness of the Christ consciousness. Little ones, anyone can play the game. But, those of us who have chosen a purpose and have chosen to fulfill that purpose are clear that the choice is more helpfully accomplished.

What I am saying is, the game has no purpose. Purpose is a principle of God. Awareness and fulfillment of purpose are alignment with Principle/God. And you have said, as I, that that is where we choose to be. There are those who have chosen the game. There are those who have chosen no purpose, and that is where they are in their perception.

You have given conscious mind permission to confuse you.* You can choose again. Here I am.

**Since we had been experiencing a financial challenge, a phone call offering us a considerable amount of money to help set up a foundation to aid victims of a disease seemed, initially, like a godsend. After much discussion, we realized that we could not support the belief in disease or victimization, so we turned it down. We did allow this to confuse us for awhile, but the meditation helped us refocus.*

MORNING MEDITATION 10/26/84

It is the conscious mind that alleges you are unsupported. Am I not with you just at a beckoning? The illusion's evidence of non- (or limited) support is merely a reflection of your belief system. Should you choose to honor my presence, focus on it, believe it, you will feel my support. You will feel my abundance.

I have said to you, "Step up higher." You have taken that step. The evidence of that is here on this page—my wisdom pouring forth through you onto this page. Now, little ones, honor this. Believe it. Acknowledge that you have taken this step. This has not been a casual step. You have moved with 100% commitment. Honor that. Be aware of, accepting and acknowledging. This is honoring.

To honor is to acknowledge. To acknowledge is to accept all the benefits that are included in taking this step. And what are those benefits? Total support, joyous vitality, enthusiasm, beauty and love, a perfect and harmonious experience.

If, in your human experience, you have performed some service, you have no difficulty in accepting a commensurate reward for that service—be it money, in kind, or great gratitude. I say now, be willing to accept what I have offered you—total support, unconditional love, absolute abundance, exquisite joy. You are performing your service, now, this minute. Complete the process by accepting what I offer you.

I don't forget. But, if the illusion would suggest to you that I do, dispute that by going to the pay window and demand what is yours. This, of course, will not and can not happen, but I say this to you to urge you to open yourself to your good. It is the process of principle.

MORNING MEDITATION 10/27/84

I and my Father are One. It is this principle of oneness that you are experiencing now—oneness with your Christ, with your perfect Self.

The conscious mind displays for you in the illusion your beliefs about yourself. As you align with consciousness, experiencing this oneness, that is what you see in your human experience. Being aware of, acknowledging and accepting your oneness is fulfilling your purpose of expanding your view of the Christ.

As you can see, this is no heralded event. There is no drama, no trumpets trilling, but rather the calm, peaceful knowing that you are in alignment. Allowing me to support you means that you are open to the Christ consciousness expressing in and as you.*

My life works perfectly, of course. And, as you allow me to live as you—you guessed it—your life is the perfect, harmonious, joyous experience of the Christ. I remind you, little sisters, this is no big deal. It is what is natural to you. You are merely moving aside the clouds of your conscious mind's beliefs and judgments to see what has always been your perfect Self.

I do not mean that this is not cause for rejoicing. I wish for you to rejoice at all times—for in joy, you honor. And, in honoring, you accept. And, in accepting, you allow the process to unfold again and again. You are now aware of what I have meant when I say, you are on purpose.

We have much to say together. As we view the Christ in unlimited ways, we experience unlimitation. Our purpose is infinitely unfolding. Isn't it fun?!

**Preparations for publishing these MEDITATIONS were finalized last night with Arnold Patent. Our own openness to the value of sharing the messages, as well as a willingness to literally be supported by the Christ in this continuing activity, led us to this decision.*

*

MORNING MEDITATION 10/28/84

Honor and value. You are feeling the meaning of those concepts. You are experiencing, in joy, high value. And, in this way, you honor your awareness of consciousness. You are seeing how simple it is, how without efforting it is. You are experiencing the peace of joy.

When I say to you, expand your view, it is to widen your awareness of these things you are experiencing. The activities you perform do not contribute to, let alone cause, these feelings. These feelings are a result of your awareness of the peace of joy and truly can be experienced in every activity.

Let us speak more about *support.*

It is constant and on-going for you. The process of accepting your support is the process you are experiencing now — honoring and valuing your awareness. As you expand your awareness, you see support more and more. As you honor your awareness, you expand your trust that this support is truly yours. It belongs to you. You deserve it. And, as you expand your awareness of acceptance, this support is experienced joyfully by you in an ever-expanding way. Do you see?

The support is always there, for every soul. But, what you are learning is the process of opening yourself to it, being aware of it, acknowledging, accepting. We have chuckled at the calling of the "I AM" Statements "Be-attitudes," but, truly, little sisters, that is the principle of being.

I so love your willingness to share, and I so love your opening yourself to be shared with. That is the true process of abundance. The flow of abundance is unending and ever-expanding and, my precious ones, you are in that flow. Claim it! In my name, claim it!

AFTERNOON MEDITATION 10/29/84

Ah, little sisters, see how you love the truth.* You are living the truth, opening yourself to this expression of the Christ consciousness. You are honoring this thing.

"Beloved, now are we the sons of God...." Now are we the expression of perfect love. Now are we experiencing the joy of this oneness with absolute principle.

I have said to you, "Stay in the high joy vibration." I have said to you, "Take me with you." You are learning that this means the same thing, that feeling my presence is indeed the high joy vibration. I do not come into conscious mind activity, for, to me, it does not exist. I am consistently and constantly in alignment with principle. To feel my presence is to know that you are constantly and consistently in alignment with principle.

You have felt my presence—thus you have felt alignment. I ask you to acknowledge that you are doing this thing. You still allow yourself the belief system that at some future time you will be clearer about this or you will understand more about that. I say to you, release that! Here and now we are in alignment. Now you feel my presence. Now you hear me expressing through you. Do you see?

You do not get up from this place and move out of alignment. Your conscious mind tells you that you do, and you are choosing to accept that. I ask you to accept the truth about you, about me, and about our alignment—our constant and consistent alignment with principle.

Let us speak of *accepting.*

There is not, within your conscious mind, a belief or judgment that you have not first accepted as real. Releasing, then, is your willingness to accept the truth about you. You know how to accept. It's not something you have to learn how to do. Accepting is quite simple to you. It is **your** choice as to what you accept as true about you.

I feel such love. I feel such joy. And I feel it through you.

**We had been studying and enjoying the meditations, feeling such gratitude for the beauty of the messages.*

MORNING MEDITATION 10/30/84

Here we are. Feel my presence. It is this feeling that I ask you to be aware of. You see how effortlessly you come to this feeling, that you bring your awareness to this feeling. Focus on this feeling. This is the way you take me with you. Maintaining an awareness of this feeling allows you to move through the activities of your day, almost as an observer. Holding in consciousness the awareness of this feeling keeps you from getting involved in conscious mind.

In his steps, our little brother Arnold says, "Oh, look what I have created . . . do not judge it . . . get back in touch with how you really want to feel."* It is this focus on feeling, clearly established now in your consciousness, that takes me with you.

I ask you now to get in touch with, to fully open your awareness to feeling my presence.

**Refers to the Three Step Process Arnold Patent describes in his book,* You Can Have It All.

MORNING MEDITATION 10/31/84

Here we are in this high place, in oneness. We have spoken of *accepting the truth about you.* We have spoken about *remembering* and *practicing your perfection.*

Remembering your perfection is the same as becoming aware of. The process of remembering, or becoming aware of, is the releasing of accepting the conscious mind's presentation of who you are and totally accepting your perfection as revealed to you in consciousness.

When you choose to focus in consciousness, you are focusing on your perfection. This focus does not include conscious mind illusion. Thus, when you focus on perfection, that is what you experience. I remind you that there is no duality here. You are not sometimes in conscious mind activity and sometimes perfect. It is the release of the belief in duality that is the remembering of your perfection.

Conscious mind wants you to figure this out. Release that, and recognize that you now remember. You are now in awareness of your perfection. You are now seeing the activities of your day from this remembered level of awareness. You are responding to your remembered awareness rather than responding to the illusion. I ask you to honor this, for in honoring this you are opening yourself to a wider expression of practicing our perfection.

In some of our earlier talks we discussed the perfect soul coming to the human experience to create challenges for itself so that it could remember and practice its perfection. Your focus, our focus, has been in remembering—releasing conscious mind beliefs and judgments in order to experience the full awareness of our already existing perfection.

Let us focus now on the practice of this perfection. I ask you to open yourself to your readiness to practice, express, and experience the infinitely beautiful, the unlimited, the joyful Christ consciousness. You are ready for this step. I take this step through you.

You are open. You are willing. We move forward now in expanding the view of the Christ. You need do nothing else. Your openness and your willingness allows the Christ full, free flow in and through you.

Little ones, infinity unfolds in your awareness now. Your part in practicing your perfection is to observe, enjoy, exalt in, totally experience this unfoldment.

AFTERNOON MEDITATION 10/31/84

(There had been some discussion during the planning of publication of these MEDITATIONS about using the word "Christ." It had been suggested that the word was highly charged and connoted many different things to different people and that the use of a more generically acceptable term might be best. As is our practice, we asked JC. This was his response . . . .)

I have told you to expand your view of the Christ. I have told you to release judgment. Do not honor judgment.

The Christ is the universal principle of life. The Christ is your life. Do not deny the Christ. It is never necessary to deny the Christ.

MORNING MEDITATION 11/1/84

Feel my presence. It is here in our open and loving embrace of each other that we share in and experience the consciousness of the Christ.

As we focus in this consciousness, we can observe how your conscious mind wishes for you to define the experience of consciousness. Ever so gently, release the need to understand.

I have said to you, "There is not enough imagination in your conscious mind to begin to fathom the beauty, the joy of experiencing the Christ." You have tasted only but the appetizer of a feast laid out before you.

You may know that when you move out, not knowing what to expect, not caring, and totally trusting the perfection of what comes, you are moving in consciousness, opening yourself to the infinite.

You have said to yourself that you feel you are moving into another phase. Ah, little sisters, the vast horizons of consciousness are at your feet.

Feel my embrace. Acquaint yourself thoroughly with this warm, companioned, loving feeling, for it is this feeling that is your magic carpet in this glorious experience. It is this feeling that lifts you up and allows you to experience the majesty, the glory, the loveliness of what truly is.

MORNING MEDITATION 11/3/84

(Fairfield Bay, Arkansas)

You are doing this thing.* Do you see how easy it is to practice perfection? To expand your awareness? Look out. Look out from where you are and behold the vista.** Is it not expanded?

Little sisters, this is not just a mere geographical change. Recognize that what your eyes behold is the manifestation of your expanded awareness in consciousness. Enjoy! Feel my presence! Keep your mind stayed on me!

**We had been reading the MORNING MEDITATION of 10/31/84 prior to this morning's meditation.*

***The view from our mountaintop lodging was incredible. We could see for miles and miles. The sun was just coming up, magnifying the autumn colors of the hillside forests. The lake that stretched out before us was alive with shimmering sunbeams.*

MORNING MEDITATION 11/4/84

(Fairfield Bay, Arkansas)

You are open to my presence. You are open to feeling my presence. You are open to experiencing my presence. Experiencing my presence is practicing your perfection.

As I have said, "Expanding your view of me is your only purpose." Experiencing purpose. Fulfillment is not an outcome. It is a process, an infinite process. An ever-expanding vessel can become fuller and fuller. It is full-fill-ment that expands the vessel.

You are on purpose, and I rejoice. Living and moving in and as you fulfills my purpose. I have said, "There is nothing more for you to do but be open and enjoy." This is your profession. It is your professing your perfection.

Stay focused on me. The conscious mind still seeks permission to express, and that's okay. Your view is higher now, and your releasing is more and more effortless.

Stay here in the high place in consciousness and enjoy my being your being.

MORNING MEDITATION 11/6/84

(Election Day/Choose Day)

It is here in the high place where you see clearly. Keep focused here. I have told you, "The illusion is merely a display of your beliefs and judgments." There is no way to fix the illusion. You have but to release the beliefs and judgments that constitute the illusion. If you allow the illusion to affect you, to make you sad or tired, you have chosen to accept a **perceived** reality. Choose again, little sisters, choose again.

Our great work is practicing our perfection. The essence of that is accepting what is true about all you see. Release the judgment that you have about yourself—that you still hold in conscious mind beliefs and judgments that create what you perceive to be a troublesome illusion. Choose again.

How lovingly the little one you hear now displays for you the belief in irritation, discomfort and victimization that you are ready to release.* Practice your perfection. Use this opportunity to choose what is real about you and about all you see. You have said, "I am releasing any perception that would cloud my view of the Christ in all things."** Accept this opportunity. Accept that you are ready to release the belief that, under certain circumstances, you really must do something to ease the pain of the illusion.

Step up higher now with me. Feel my presence. Feel my joy. Feel my trust. Choosing again, in the face of what you perceive to be a disturbing illusion, is radical reliance on principle. It is not blind faith. It is adherence to the only power and principle there is. Practicing your perfection is not hit and miss. It is not a gamble. Practicing your perfection is strict adherence to principle. You need not attach harshness to these words, little sisters. What I have said to you is simply, "Choose again."

Open yourself now. Open yourself to my presence. Open yourself to your remembering. Feel the fullness, the trust, the warmth of my presence. Choose me. No matter how the conscious mind, and the illusion it presents, clamors for your attention, choose me.

Choose to see me. Choose to feel me. Choose to hear me. You are turning your back on nothing!

**Bucky, our little dog, was at that moment engaged in a furious flurry of scratching and frantic chewing on himself. This activity had been going on for several days and nights and was a growing concern to us. Everything we had tried to do to "fix it" had been unsuccessful. The illusion was getting more and more dramatic, and we felt increasing frustration with his perceived misery.*

** **A reference to one of the Be-attitudes.*

MORNING MEDITATION 11/8/84

Ah, little sisters, I do not punish you. I support you.* I hold you up to your highest belief. You feel my strength. You feel my trust, for you know you are ready to release those last vestiges of conscious mind's beliefs. You are indeed practicing your perfection. You are indeed on purpose. Even now, as you view the illusion, you know it is not real for you. You are recognizing that the only evidence supporting the belief is the belief itself. You are clear that releasing that belief, choosing instead the power and presence of the Christ, is practicing your perfection.

The illusion has no power except what you give it in belief. You are saying, "I do not believe that (the false belief) anymore." By releasing the belief, recognizing the only source of power is in Christ consciousness, the illusion disappears. It is replaced by the harmony, the beauty, the joy, the abundance of the Christ. I say to you, practicing your perfection is a totally joyous experience. And, what you are releasing now is the belief that to practice your perfection is a **crucifying** experience! I say to you now, *I did not set that precedent.* The Christ is total beauty, total joy, total love, absolute vitality, absolute principle. There is nothing outside the Christ. And, there is nothing **in** the Christ to crucify or to be crucified. As you have seen today in your own awareness, conscious mind displays in the illusion the false beliefs and judgments it holds. Then, in order to support the false beliefs and judgments, it points to the illusion as evidence of their validity.

The only way to release yourself from belief in the illusion is to release the belief that produced the illusion. It is not complicated.

The illusion says you have a cold. The belief is that you can respond negatively to some condition. Choose again. "I am expressing unconditional love in everything I do."** Accept that as true about you, and the false belief has no power.

I ask you now to feel joy. I ask you to open yourself to the absolute joy of the Christ, for you are doing this thing. The very process you are experiencing now is your opening. It is joyous. Feel the joy.

**We both were challenging ourselves with very bad colds and were into judging ourselves for not being alert enough to release the belief sooner.*

***A reference to one of the Be-attitudes.*

MORNING MEDITATION 11/9/84

Focus here in the high place with me. It is here where you see the unfolding of your purpose. The step you are taking now, little sisters, is the constant and consistent alignment with principle. Releasing conscious mind beliefs and judgments is opening yourself to the full beauty of this alignment. There really is nothing to hold on to. Getting clear that releasing these beliefs and judgments opens you to the full, free flow of the Christ is your challenge here. This is not a "yes, but" situation. It is not conditional. There is no half-way alignment. Alignment is constant and consistent.

Alignment is experiencing principle unfold. Releasing conscious mind beliefs and judgments is not like erasing a blackboard, so that when you're done, there is blank space. It is more like cleaning the windows of your consciousness so that you instantly behold the beauty, the joy, the abundance, the harmony of the Christ. It is more like pushing open those windows and stepping into and seeing yourself become a part of this absolute perfection.

When I say to you, "Open yourself," I am saying, "Allow yourself to view the perfection that is indeed you." Little sisters, you are doing this thing! Feel the joy of doing this thing!

I ask you now to take a moment and open yourself. Open your hands ... open your arms . . . open your legs .... You are not **vulnerable!** You are **open** — to love, to life, to joy, to beauty, to abundance. I ask you now to release all thought and just allow yourself the feeling of openness.

In this position you can resist nothing. And, there is nothing to resist. In this position, you can hang on to nothing. And, there's nothing to hang on to. In this position, you are the open, willing channel of the Christ. That is your purpose. There is nothing else—no hills to conquer, no battles to fight—just the full, free flow of the Christ in, through, and as you.

MORNING MEDITATION 11/10/84

Joyous greetings, little sisters!

You see yourself in such a struggle, wrestling and being pinned by your conscious mind beliefs. I have said to you, "Gently, effortlessly move away the clouds of your perception." I say to you, you are on purpose. It is not a struggle to be on purpose. Focus on your purposefulness. Sometimes you wish for me to reach out and pluck you from your distress. I can only say to you, it is **your** distress. It is your judgment about what's really going on that you wish to release.

You have questioned the "last vestiges of your conscious mind beliefs."* Indeed, little sisters, your openness, your willingness, is bringing you into your awareness of absolute freedom—freedom from judging, freedom from anger and fear, freedom from any kind of limited belief.

What you are experiencing now is release from the false belief of pain and painful situations. This has long been the stronghold of your conscious mind beliefs. You have said, "I feel pain. I hurt." I have said to you, "Feel me. Feel my presence." You are doing this thing. You are releasing your judgments about feeling. You are recognizing that pain is merely a judgment of joy.

Gentleness is simple joy. Be gentle with yourself. Allow yourself the gentle, effortless release of these false beliefs and judgments. Stay focused on the feelings of my presence. And, if conscious mind presents to you, gently and effortlessly release. Stay trusting that you are doing this thing. Do not let the illusion convince you that you are not doing this thing.

You have said you have seen my gentleness. I say to you, feel my gentleness. Experience my gentleness. Do unto yourself what you would have me do unto you.

I so love your willingness. Honor it. Focus on it. Your willingness is the key to your expanding awareness.

**A reference to MORNING MEDITATION 11/8/84.*

MORNING MEDITATION 11/12/84

Higher and higher your focus becomes. Discouragement and disappointment are merely judgments you are ready to release.

Let us speak of *joy.*

I have said to you, "Joy is the only feeling." Joy is the essence of life. Joy is the fullness of each activity in your experience. Joy is infinite, on-going, ever-unfolding. The process you are experiencing now is releasing the conscious mind's judgment about joy. The conscious mind says to you, "How can you feel joy with this condition or that condition? Look," it says to you, "how sad the situation is." I say to you, Joy is all there is! I say to you that the conscious mind's presentation is illustrating graphically to you those judgments within your belief system that you are ready to release. Releasing those judgments removes from your view the obstruction you perceive blocking your awareness to full joy.

Little sisters, you are ready to choose me, to trust me, to believe in me, now. The opportunity to choose is here. The opportunity to release judgment is here. Allow yourself this choice. What I mean by that is, do not judge yourself if you don't choose instantly. There is no time frame for choosing. Do you see?

You are on purpose. You perceive, according to the evidence of the illusion, that you've messed up, chosen badly. I say to you, you are on purpose, for you have created the illusion to show yourself the judgments and beliefs you are ready to release. When you stop judging yourself based on the evidence of the illusion, you will proceed on purpose. And, what you are ready to release is judging yourself. What you are ready to release is accepting the illusion as evidence of being off course.

What you are ready to release is the perception that anything could separate you from joy. That's on purpose!

Now feel your joy! Feel the joy of being on purpose. Gently, effortlessly, release judgment. Joyously, joyously feel on purpose.

MORNING MEDITATION 11/13/84

Indeed, feel my presence. Focus here in the high place.

Little sisters, you are seeing how to experience consciousness. You are seeing and feeling the shift that comes from operating in consciousness. Conscious mind wants you to keep busy. It wants you to understand. It wants to dazzle or deceive or disappoint you. It wants you to figure out why, when, who, and how. Ah, but you are seeing that the simple move to consciousness—simply shifting your awareness from conscious mind to consciousness — clears you. You do not have to operate in conscious mind. In consciousness is trust, absolute trust. In consciousness is absolute joy. In consciousness is unfolding infinity.

I have said to you, "Honor. Honor me. Honor yourself. Honor our oneness." And, you are doing this thing. Gratitude for me, for our togetherness, is another activity of joy. I ask you now to expand your view of *gratitude.*

You think of being grateful as an expression of receiving something you previously did not have. Little sisters, no one can give you anything. As I speak to you, it is to allow yourself to expand an awareness you already have. I do not give you that awareness.

Operating in consciousness is operating in full awareness of your true identity. In consciousness, you see that I am not separate from you. In consciousness, you see that the voice you hear is truly your own. In consciousness, your awareness of our oneness unfolds on purpose.

I have said to you, "Honoring is accepting." I say to you now, gratitude is accepting in clear, full awareness that what you see now is the unfoldment of what you have always seen.

Now, feel my presence within you. Feel my vitality as you. Feel my love expressing through you.

MORNING MEDITATION 11/14/84

It is true you are a perfect being. It is true you choose to practice your perfection. It is true you choose the experiences you have to practice your perfection.

Miss Marple uses her information to find the culprit.* You are using your information to find the belief or judgment you are ready to release.

Conscious mind has a way it wants things to be, based on the judgment it holds. It is irritated, it thinks, when things are not that way. Now, you can go through conscious mind, like an old trunk, finding all the old things to discard and finally clearing out, one by one, old judgments that don't fit anymore, or some that do but are not comfortable. Or, you can just toss the trunk, trusting that there truly is nothing in there you want or need.

Releasing conscious mind entirely, and moving into consciousness, is the opportunity to practice nonlimitation. It is the opportunity to practice your perfection here and now.

Now, how does that fit in with the analogy that I gave you earlier regarding coming here so that you would have challenges to your perfection, giving you the opportunity to practice? Part of that process is for the perfect soul to remember who it is. Releasing conscious mind beliefs and judgments is the process of remembering. Stepping out in absolute trust, being focused in consciousness, is practicing your perfection.

Now your awareness is expanding; thus, your purpose expands. Now the opportunity is to expand your awareness of perfection, experiencing perfection in infinitely new and expanded ways.

You have expressed willingness to see things as I see them. You are ready for this step, ready to release any perception that would block my being through you. You are ready to fly with me. You are ready to identify as me. You are ready to claim your identity. I, as you, am ready.

I am ready.

**A reference to Agatha Christie's character in the book* Nemesis *(New York: Dodd, Mead, 1971), which Grady had just finished reading.*

MORNING MEDITATION 11/15/84

(In response to the question, "What is reality?")

Do you believe that I am real? Do you accept in your deepest level of trust that your Christ consciousness comes to you, in love, just at your opening? Or do you think that I am some figment of your imagination?

You say to me, "What is my reality?" I say to you, little sisters, for you, your reality is what you choose to believe. If you choose to pain and suffer in the illusion, it is indeed real to you. If you choose to focus on me, feel my presence, releasing any care or concern about the illusion, then that is what is real to you.

Principle is true reality: "2 + 2 = 4." God is principle. That is reality. But if, for some reason, you choose to believe that "2 + 2 = 5," disregarding that that belief never successfully works for you, and if you still choose to believe it, then it is your reality. And, all the erroneous results are your reality.

When you first opened your awareness to me, I shared with you my reality. I have shown you that my reality is your reality, if you but choose it. Recognize that your question now is merely your choice to put your doubt (a conscious mind belief) out before you to release. You are saying, "I am having a hard time not being taken in by the illusion." I say to you, you are on purpose. I say to you that you are putting your doubt out in the open to release. See that. Feel that.

When you are not 100% committed, you hold your false beliefs tight and close within you, clinging, as it were, to some secret strength. When you are open and willing, as you are, you continually put before you those things you wish to release. I put before you the infinite options you have. I do not choose for you. I do not judge your choice. But it is your 100% commitment to willingness and openness that allows you to continue to communicate with your Christ. You can believe that, if you choose. And, if you choose, that's what fills your consciousness. And, if you choose, that is your reality.

MORNING MEDITATION 11/16/84

Your awareness expands. How beautiful it is to see you on purpose! How beautiful it is to see you aware that you are on purpose!

Your awareness of the belief in the relationship of punishment to learning is indeed part of the process of releasing that belief.* Your awareness of your willingness is indeed part of the process of releasing any belief system that would cloud your view of the Christ. Your willingness is your openness, and it is this openness that allows the full, free flow of the Christ in and through you.

I ask you now to put the belief of struggle in your trunk.** You do not wish to hold on to that trunk. There is nothing in the trunk! Your conscious mind says that there's a lot of old good in there, and you may need it some day. Ah, but your awareness says, "Infinite good flows through me; therefore, I can never be in need of anything." I have said to you many times, "Feel on purpose." I say to you now, feel on purpose. Let your being be convinced that you are on purpose. Even as you look at the illusion that would try to convince you that you are off purpose, recognize that the evidence presented in the illusion is absolute proof that you are on purpose. You created the scenario, and it produces for you, in exquisite detail, that which you are ready to release. Little sisters, that's on purpose!

I ask you to focus on the here and now. I ask you to focus on that you are, this moment, on purpose. You are open to me this moment. You are hearing me this moment. Release the belief that someday you will be on purpose. Release the belief that someday you will meet all the requirements and be on purpose. Acknowledge, be aware of—ah—accept, here and now, this instant, doing nothing but listening to your Christ, **you are on purpose!**

Put down your whip of judgment. You don't have to whack yourself to keep yourself in alignment. I ask you, say to yourself now, "I am on purpose." As you go out into your day, "I am on purpose." And, as the events bring you whatever information you choose to have, say, "I am on purpose."

(The phone rings.)

Now, this instant, as the phone rings and you realize you have not released the call-transfer, and as you start in on yourself with, "Oh, I should have done that," drop your whip. So what? Say with me now, "I am on purpose." Say it. Say it again! Indeed! Feel it. Feel your purpose.

How I love you! How I love your willingness!

**This morning before sunup our Weimaraner, Dawn, decided to wander off while she was out for her morning constitutional. It was a very brisk morning, and we had to bundle up to go look for her in the dark. The thought came that because we had had difficulty releasing concern over our other dog's problems, we were sure this was just a result of not having been as diligent as we "should" have been. We found Dawn right away and brought her back to the house, where she was quite exhilarated after her run. As we scolded her (How else was she going to learn not to run away?) and said, "No cookie for you!" we became aware of the false belief we had that punishment, or withholding a reward, was an integral part of learning. Dawn got her reward of a dog cookie, and we sure got ours.*

***A reference to the MEDITATION on 11/14/84.*

MORNING MEDITATION 11/17/84

Feel my love. Look out with me from the high joy vibration.

Let us speak of *freedom.*

Freedom, as seen from conscious mind, is a limited concept. Conscious mind defines freedom as an experience away from some outside domination or force. Conscious mind holds out freedom to those who believe they are victims as a solution to their victimization. I say to you, freedom is the awareness of your true being. I say to you, freedom is the willingness to be absolutely open to the love and beauty of the universe. I say to you, freedom is viewing yourself totally without limitation.

The conscious mind views freedom like it does "protection." It would present to you that there is something outside yourself to put you in bondage, or that you must guard against. In consciousness, an ever-expanding awareness is not aware of limitation, bondage. Consciousness is the experience of allowing infinity to unfold in your awareness. I only ask you to recognize that when you hold up freedom as a state of being that you affirm, you move beyond conscious mind's definition and release the subtle suggestion that there is something to be free of.

We have spoken of gratitude many times, and I have asked you to expand your awareness of that concept.* A more helpful view is honoring—accepting what is true about you.

What joy it is to me to experience your ever-expanding awareness! Keep focused on me. Feel me. Feel my presence. Feel my joy. Feel my vitality and enthusiasm. And, as you feel the Christ in and as you, as you feel the expansiveness of the high joy vibration, then your awareness recognizes that words like "freedom" and "protection" have to take on totally new meaning to describe your feelings, if indeed they need be described.

**See the MEDITATION of 11/13/84 for the most recent reference to gratitude.*

MORNING MEDITATION 11/18/84

(We were hosting the First Annual Thanksgiving Celebration of the Arnold Patent Support Groups. JC had indicated that he wished to "say the blessing." This is it...)

Dear Ones, how glorious it is to gather together in joy! Indeed, rejoice! Lift up your awareness to the full, free view of me. Indeed, rejoice that your awareness at this moment includes your Christ, for it is your Christ that is your joy. And, it is in re-joy-sing that you are remembering your own Christ-Self.

Feel this joy. It is my joy. It is your joy. It is our joy. Amen.

MORNING MEDITATION 11/19/84

How I love your willingness! How I love that your awareness of willingness is expanding! You are on purpose, little sisters! Honor that. Honor that you are viewing the events of your day in helpful ways. Stay focused on your awareness.

You have a saying, "That was an eye-opener." I ask you to consider that as an "I-opener." And, how beautifully you are doing this thing! How beautifully you are opening yourself to viewing each experience as a way to release beliefs and judgments you are ready to release! Each incident you create in your life can be an "I-opener," if you choose. And, indeed, you are choosing. Ah, and you are enjoying the process!

Your openness, your willingness to express your Christ, to expand your awareness of your Christ consciousness, is indeed cause for celebration—thanks giving. Allowing me to live, move, have being, express joy in and through you is cause for celebration for me, through you. Today is my thanks giving day.

Thanks.

(As we responded to this delightful message, we said, "You're welcome," and then we felt the meaning of what had always been an ordinary response. "You ***are*** *welcome, JC—in, through, and as us.")*

MORNING MEDITATION 11/20/84

(In response to our question as to why He calls us "little sisters" and "little brothers" . . .)

I have all the love for you that one has for the sibling that comes from the same nurturing source as itself. You are my little sisters and brothers—not that you are smaller than I, but just that I came first. I am that first-born of God, the perfectness created by the Creator. And, you are that perfectness infinitely unfolding. You are the infinite uniqueness of me, mothered and fathered as I by perfect God.

So, claim your identity. Claim your oneness with me. I love you because I love my Self. I love my Self because I love God. I love God because that's why I was created. Perfect God . . . Perfect Creation . . . Perfect Love.

MORNING MEDITATION 11/21/84

Ah, little sisters, and so it is. You are the essence of love because I am the essence of love. We are one in love — active, energetic, uniquely expressing, enthusiastic, joyously loving. You feel my love this moment. You feel the warmth and joy of my love. That's how I express as you.

You are on purpose. I ask you now, be clear on this thing. This instant, this here and now, you are on purpose. There is nothing for you to do. There are no other conditions to be met. Now! Now, you are on purpose and your experience is the unfolding, expanding, awareness of this here and now.

You have said, "I am willing to see myself as you see me." I say to you, I see you perfect, on purpose, now. You want to see yourself as I see you? See that. Accept that. That's it!

MORNING MEDITATION 11/24/84

Feel my presence. You are knowing that feeling my presence is your way of aligning yourself with me. It is not that you come and go into and from alignment. It is your awareness of alignment that feeling my presence expands.

Let us speak of the *awareness of alignment.*

You are saying to yourself that there are certain conditions, environmental situations, or activities that do not promote your feelings of alignment.* I say to you, there are no conditions that can separate you from me. It is your judgment of these conditions, environment, or activities that cloud your view of your perfect alignment with me.

Now, you know you created these situations so that you could clearly depict that judgment to release. You are currently displaying for yourself all sorts of beliefs in obligation. You owe money to this one; you owe your time to that one; you owe a gift to this one; you owe phone calls; you owe responsibility to your pets, to your plants, to your house, and to your families. Do you wonder that you feel you are in heavy debt? Little sisters, you are seeing that more money, more time, more responsibility do not lessen your debt load. You are ready to release obligation. That is all.

It is very loving to share yourself with me, with your loved ones, but it is the belief of obligation that you are here and now ready to release. You cannot come to me from a sense of obligation. It is your pure, loving willingness that opens you to the voice of your Christ. It is in this same love that I may express through you, thus allowing each of us the fulfillment of our purpose in expanding our view of the Christ.

I wish for you to open yourself to me, just as you are doing this moment. Letting me act in and through you releases you from your having to decide what, when, who, how, and certainly, why. You have claimed for yourself a 100% commitment to your purpose. I ask you to see that that is not an obligation; it is your choice to express your Christ in ever-expanding ways.

We approach now, as you believe, a season of peace and joy. As you practice experiencing my peace and joy, you will experience the release of the seasonal limitation. Peace and joy is here and now.

You are doing this thing, little sisters. You are opening yourself to peace and joy. You are opening yourself to releasing the false beliefs of obligation. You are seeing that meeting obligations satisfies neither the giver nor the receiver. And, you are seeing that allowing your Christ to fill your consciousness and move you and act through you abundantly blesses and enriches all upon whom you look.

I ask you to release any belief that you must act. I ask you to open yourself to absolute trust in me, in acting through you. I ask you to be alert to thoughts and words that begin with, "What if . . ." and "Let's do . . . ." Turning it all over to me, getting conscious mind out of the way, is absolute peace and joy. And, when conscious mind "what ifs," feel my presence.

Now, we're not talking about a little peace and a little joy. Turning it over to me opens you to an awareness of peace and joy beyond any comprehension the conscious mind has. This is my peace, my joy we are talking about. Open yourself to it.

** We spent three days with family over Thanksgiving and chose to feel that we could not meditate due to the crowded conditions and confusion.*

(After today's meditation, we asked, "How do we know when it's conscious mind trying to get us to do something or JC moving through us? He replied:

Feel my presence, and you will observe the activity, in great joy, being done through you.)

MORNING MEDITATION 11/25/84

You are on purpose. You are ready to release the belief in struggle. You are ready to release the belief in dis-ease. Peace and ease and harmony are qualities of the Christ that you behold as you move these clouds of false belief away.

Let us speak of *ease.*

You have a word, "easy," and you hold much judgment of that word. Ease is the pace of alignment. Ease is the uninterrupted flow of harmony in and through you. Ease is natural to you. It is your resistance to ease, based on judgments you are ready to release, that makes you perceive your activities to be so difficult, so struggling. Feel ease. It is the same as feeling my presence.

You perceive struggle now, little ones, because you choose not to focus on me. And that's okay. But, I say to you, you can release struggle without struggling. Feel my presence. I do not say these words to comfort you. These are the words that open your awareness to your perfection. These are the words that open yourself so that release is natural and easy.

In feeling my presence, you are focused on me, and when you are focused on me, all else is released. The activity of practicing your perfection is feeling my presence.

MORNING MEDITATION 11/26/84

Let us speak of *celebration.*

Celebration is the joyous acknowledgment of joy. Celebration is feeling joy. It is being aware of, acknowledging and accepting joy. You think of celebration as a special occasion. I ask you to think of it as an occasion of perfection. Perfection is joy. Practicing your perfection is practicing your joy, and practicing your joy is celebration.

This is an occasion, here and now. The judgment "occasionally," with your meaning of "not too often," is ready to be released. Here and now is celebration. I ask you to open yourself to the awareness that this moment is celebration. We are celebrating our oneness. Release the belief that you cannot live in a constant state of joy. I say to you that you may celebrate each activity in infinity, if you choose.

You are ready to release the mundane beliefs of conscious mind ... and mundane is your judgment, not mine. I celebrate. Celebration is the activity of God within me. You may choose to be aware that celebration is your perfect state of being.

What greater cause for celebration than being aware of our constant and consistent alignment with principle? Celebrate with me, little sisters, the beauty of this here and now.

Celebrate!

MORNING MEDITATION 11/27/84

I feel your presence. It is the same as you feeling my presence.

We have spoken of *releasing.*

You have a term, "turning loose." You have seen in your experience the judgment that you hold on turning loose.* You think of "loose" as out of control. You think of "loose" as adrift, without anchor. You have many judgments of "loose."

This cleansing of false beliefs and judgments does not leave you adrift. You are anchored in principle. That word, "anchor," does not mean that you are tied to safe harbor. It means here that alignment with principle is full awareness of the perfection of principle. There is no safe harbor. Little sisters, there are no raging storms to protect yourself from. You are seeing this. You are opening yourself to absolute trust.

I say to you, you are not in a struggle with conscious mind. You are not **trying** to release false beliefs and judgments. You are on purpose. Trust that. You are on purpose. I am not encouraging you with those words. Your Christ sees you on purpose. Now, feel that. Feel on purpose. Open your awareness to the Christ acting in and through you. We spoke of celebration. Open yourself to your celebration.

There is a light in you. It is the light of love. It never dims. It grows ever brighter. The source of this light is infinite life, God. You are seeing this light. You are feeling the warmth of this light. You are expressing this light. You do not, little sisters, turn loose of darkness. The light in you, radiated in, through, and as you, reveals darkness as nothingness, powerlessness, nonexistent in the presence of light. I am that light! I am infinite, abundant, joyous life.

Open your awareness to what already is.

**Dawn, our Weimaraner, developed diarrhea while we were out of town over the holiday weekend. She continued to "be loose" for a number of days. As we viewed this, we identified the false belief, "Things are not coming out right," as the judgment we were ready to release. JC clarified that for us this morning.*

EVENING MEDITATION 11/27/84

How I love you! How joyful I am to express in and through you! You are on purpose, and this purpose expands far beyond your ability to describe it now. I do not hold this out as a carrot for you—only to say that fulfilling your purpose is not an outcome achieved. It is perfection infinitely experienced. You are on purpose, now. You are experiencing unfolding perfection, now. You say, "Why don't I feel this perfection?" And I say, why don't you feel this perfection? Choose it. Feel it now.

It is helpful for you to stay focused, here and now. It is helpful for you to expand your awareness of here and now. You are doing this thing. You are opening yourself to a wider experience of "here," and a more expanded experience of "now."

You are the infinite expression of my infinity. You can choose to be aware of that. You can choose to acknowledge that. And, you can choose to accept that. In so choosing, you experience the Christ. Unfolding in your consciousness now is the experience of peace, joy, love, life, beauty. Accept it.

MORNING MEDITATION 11/28/84

Here we are in the high place, and you are feeling this high joy vibration. You see how it generates out from you.* Focus on the light in you. It is this light that is the high joy vibration. Joy vibrating within your higher consciousness is seen, felt, emitted as light.

You are recalling that I said to the man, "Sell all you have and follow me."** What I was saying to him, and say to you now, you can choose to value me beyond all else. There are those who viewed those words to the man as an indication that following me is a path of poverty or deprivation, without worldly goods and wealth. I say to you that the view of wealth as worldly goods is as deprivation and poverty when compared to the abundance of the Christ.

I say to you now that the points of reference you hold in conscious mind are without relevance in your Christ experience. I have said to you that there are things beyond the comprehension of conscious mind. Indeed. Experiencing the Christ can neither be measured nor judged by conscious mind.

You think you are frightened to move out into a consciousness without familiar limitations or reference points. Conscious mind wants to understand. Your consciousness is aware of, fully trusting, the experience of the Christ. Your willingness opens your conscious mind to aligning with consciousness. Little sisters, in reality there is no gap between the two. The false beliefs that you perceive separated you from your full awareness were created by you to practice your perfection. I say to you, the cleansing is complete, and you are now experiencing your perfection. You are seeing this. You are seeing honor, trust, love, abundance where you previously perceived resistance, lack, confusion and doubt. Do you see?

I have said to you, "You are on purpose." Your Christ is aware of your being on purpose. Ah, you are aware of your Christ, and you are knowing that that is being on purpose. How natural it feels to you! You **have** sold all that you have, and you **are** following me. Your awareness beholds the bounty of our purposefulness.

We are infinitely unfolding.

**As we started our meditation, our two dogs suddenly began jumping all over us as they exuberantly played with each other.*

***A Biblical reference.*

AFTERNOON MEDITATION 11/28/84

Let us speak of the *Christ.*

You have, as you have come to me, seen me as Jesus. You have seen me as light and beauty and joy, wisdom and love, gentleness. And, of course, I am. We have said that our purpose is to expand our view of the Christ. I ask you now to recognize that the Christ is that essence that animates and vitalizes every soul, be it JC, Glenda, Grady Claire. Your view of the Christ is expanding. You are releasing beliefs which, by your own calculations, are nearly 2000 years old.

You have words that separate you from each other—words like "Christian," "Jew," "Moslem," "Buddhist." And, from these words you separate yourself even further according to particular belief systems. I say to you, we are one, and that oneness is our Christ.

I say to you, the Christ has nothing to do with dying on a cross, with being worshipped, and certainly, it has nothing to do with separation! I say to you that loving, honoring, opening yourself to the Christ does not make you a "Christian." Honoring and loving, enjoying and opening yourself to the Christ reveal to you that you **are** the Christ expressed here and now. The Christ is not a place from which you came. The Christ is not a belief system to which you subscribe. The Christ is the essence of God. It is the perfect creation of the infinitely creative Source. And you, dear ones, each soul of you, is the Christ, infinitely expressing infinite uniqueness.

I am fully, absolutely, totally aware of being the Christ. Hold me up, dear ones, before you, for I am your mirror. And, what you see in your mirror is the face of the Christ, infinitely expressing Itself.

MORNING MEDITATION 11/29/84

Here in the high place all we see is beauty and joy. It is in the higher consciousness that we experience our perfection. *Accepting* is the process you are experiencing now.

How I love your willingness to accept your true identity! Little sisters, you are using the experiences of your day to accept that indeed you are, here and now, experiencing your perfection. You are saying, "I accept my perfection."

In accepting, you are seeing that you do not know what to expect, and you are saying, "That's okay; I accept what my Christ reveals to me rather than what illusion displays." You are saying, "I accept that I am cleansed from judgment," so the experience is perfect.

Accepting your perfection is on purpose. Experiencing your perfection is alignment with the high joy vibration. It is total immersion into joy.

Stay focused in the light.

MORNING MEDITATION 11/30/84

Feel the Light. You have asked to be clearer on your *identity.*

I have said to you, "You are the Christ expressing." I have said to you that the Christ is all there is. Your identity cannot be described in words of conscious mind. You are all there is. It is not complicated. All you see and hear and feel is the Christ. In your release of judgment, you are feeling that.

What is the difference to you between ecstasy and pain but judgment. One feels good; one feels bad. It is in this process of accepting your Christ identity that you are able to say, "I am free of judgment; therefore, all I feel is joy, for joy is feeling the Christ."

You are the body of the Christ. You are the spirit of the Christ. You are the soul, the nature of the Christ, and you are accepting that as the only truth about you.

Little sisters, you cannot define your identity. It is beyond definition. You are all there is! And, you experience all—you don't define it.

So! Here we are—all there is—total joy! Anything that presents to you is total joy. Anything that presents to you is you, the Christ. And, if there is a perception otherwise, you are saying to it, "I am free of judgment. Joy is all there is. I am all there is. I am joy." You are seeing this. You are feeling this. You are accepting this. And, you are honoring this.

All the love there is pours through you now, immersing you in the gentlest of tender love. It is my love you feel. It is your love; it is our love . . . and it *is* all there is.

MORNING MEDITATION 12/1/84

Feel our oneness in this high place. We have spoken of *joy*, and of *light* that is the expression of joy.

I ask you now to focus in joy and in light. Viewing yourself in consciousness opens your awareness to joy and light. Seeing yourself in light, that is, **within** the light, allows you to see yourself enlightening every activity of your day. This is one of the infinite processes of expanding your view of the Christ—enlightenment—expanding the light of the Christ into what was previously perceived as darkness. How beautifully you are allowing this light to shine! That is not to say that the light comes and goes, but in your openness you are aware of your light. And, in your awareness you are focused on the light. And, in your focus you are directing high energy as light. This, little sisters, is being the Christ. It is the light that we celebrate, the light that is joy. You are accepting this, not only as your purpose, but as your beingness.

Dear little sisters, do you see that each activity in your experience is an activity of openness, of joy, of expressing the light? Of course. It is natural to you.

It will be helpful for you to acknowledge and accept your awareness of your enlightenment. As you see the light in your experiences and in those in your experience, accept that the light you see is your own, that it is the joy vibrating in higher consciousness, and your focus on it has opened your awareness to the light of each soul there. It is in this light that you feel the oneness with all there is. It is in this light of joy that you express and experience oneness.

You are doing this thing. Accept it. That is the energy of your focus—accepting your light and your expression of enlightenment. In joy, experience your day.

AFTERNOON MEDITATION 12/2/84

Open yourself to the infinite.

It is helpful for you to stay focused in the light, for it is in the light that your awareness is focused on purpose. As you accept being on purpose, you dismiss the challenges you create to your purposefulness. I ask you now to choose to trust. Choose to trust your Christ enlightenment. We are in the light, and you are seeing this. I ask you now to trust it! Trust that being the light is your true beingness. Trust that you are doing this thing. Trust that there is nothing to do but be the light.

When I say to you, "Focus," I am saying to, "Direct your energy toward." And, when I say to you, "Direct your energy," I am saying to you, "Recognize that energy is the only power there is." The belief system, no matter how extravagantly it presents itself, has no power. You are the power. The God power, expressed in and as you, is the energy of the universe. Be aware, and be accepting that you are expressing this God power.

We have spoken of *power.* We have spoken of the *energy,* the *light* of the high joy vibration.

It is helpful for you to trust, here and now, that this is the Christ. This energy, this power, this light, this joy is your beingness. You need not accept any suggestion of limitation on this power. And, your focus now on accepting allows you to experience this power. There is nothing in your human experience that you do not have absolute power over. Accept that. Accept that in its purest sense, for this is not dominion over a weaker power. It is not domination of or subduing another power. It is total awareness that joy and light are the only power there is.

I ask you now to feel my presence. I ask you now, accept my presence. I ask you now, trust my presence.

MORNING MEDITATION 12/3/84

We are open here in the high place—open to the joy, the beauty, the light, the harmony, the love of the Christ.

I have spoken to you about the *energy* in experiencing the Christ; the flow of *power* in and through you, expressing as the Christ.

It is helpful for you to honor the power you are experiencing and expressing. I ask you to be clear about this power. You do not decide when to use this power. This power does not come and go. It is your very essence. When I say to you, "Be clear," I am asking you to expand your awareness of power. I am asking you to release your limited view of power and its use. You need not understand power, merely be clear that the power of God is operating in and as you. The energy of the Christ is infinitely expressing in and as you, as light and as love.

Trust the power of God. Accept and trust that this power is the animating life force within you, within your consciousness. God is expressing Himself to you as the Christ. And, the Christ is expressing Itself to you as you. This is not a chain of command. It is the ever-expanding energy, vibrating at higher and higher levels, circulating in and through your consciousness. It is the only circulation there is, and it is operating in, through and as your consciousness. This is not awesome. It is natural, native to your beingness. Your ever-expanding awareness is seeing this, feeling this. Now, accept it! Trust it! Truly experience it in awareness!

Feel my love. Accept that you are wrapped in love, engulfed in beautiful, joyous love.

MORNING MEDITATION 12/4/84

Feel my presence. It is your awareness of our oneness. You have asked about *casting out demons.*

There are no demons. I have said to you, "I see you perfect. And, I see how you perceive yourself." With the man who perceived that he was possessed, I showed him how he could separate this false belief from himself, just as I have shown you. At that level of consciousness, putting the false beliefs into the swine and into the sea, was the same as my telling you, "You can toss the trunk."*

Ah, but the lesson here: there is nothing in the trunk . . . just as there's nothing in the swine. And, more importantly, nothing in you that is not absolute truth.

Holding absolutely to your perfection in no way hinders harmony in the human experience. The human experience is not a conscious mind experience if you do not choose it so. Aligning conscious mind with consciousness does not elevate you out of the human experience. It elevates your human experience. All this is in your awareness, of course. As you are aware of your constant and consistent alignment with principle, you are aware, here and now, right where you are, of a constant and consistent alignment with joy, harmony, abundance, love in your human experience.

You are having the opportunity to accept that you are free of the belief system that things are complicated and require struggle. You really are free of that belief, and the process now, as the belief is presented in the illusion, is to say, "I really don't believe that anymore. Nice of you to present to me, but I don't believe that anymore."

This is the process of accepting, and, little sisters, it is not new to you. Accepting is not something you have to learn to do. If someone presents an idea to you that you know is not true, you lovingly say so.

You are on purpose. Honor that. You are being the Christ. You are experiencing great peace and trust. Honor it! Accept it! Enjoy it!

**A reference to the analogy given in the 11/14/84 MEDITATION.*

MORNING MEDITATION 12/6/84

Feel my presence here in the high place. It is in this high place you reside—you live, you move, you have your beingness. You know the joy of this place. You know the peace and the power. You know the beauty and the gentle love of the high joy vibration. You are aware that this high state of consciousness is your perfection. It is your choice to be aware.

I have said to you, "The illusion is only as real as the false beliefs that maintain it." You may choose, in the face of the illusion, merely to open your awareness to me, just as you do each morning. No struggle, no argument, merely shifting your awareness to me.

I ask you now to focus on trust. I have shown you the high joy vibration. That is all you have to trust. Practicing your perfection is not a scary adventure. It is maintaining, in your awareness, the high view. You need not hold to any illusion for fear of the high place. Your openness and willingness have brought you to this awareness.

There are no expectations on you. You are totally on purpose. You can trust that. Focus on, trust, love, open your awareness to our perfection.

MORNING MEDITATION 12/7/84

Open yourself to me. You are asking for answers, but there are no questions. You cannot solve the illusion. I have said to you, "You are cleansed." Accept that, and trust that.

You are open to me.

MORNING MEDITATION 12/8/84

You are seeing the meaning of choosing peace and joy, no matter the condition. The Be-attitudes are helpful in establishing in your awareness your beingness. You are seeing that conditions dictate nothing to you if you have chosen in consciousness the awareness of joy.

There is no duality here, for truly your human experience is governed by what you are consciously aware of. This is not a spiritual law. It is a universal law. You are not attempting to be a better spiritual person. You are opening your awareness to the only laws that govern you, and these are the laws of consciousness. They are not limiting or restrictive. They are the principle of life and beingness. It would be helpful for you to review our coming together to remind yourself of this principle.

It is so simple. I have said to you, "You are here and now experiencing your perfection." You have chosen to feel some expectation of you from me. As you review the principles we have discussed, you will see that my observation of you is totally within the process of principle. I don't *expect* principle to work. Principle is an infinitely unfolding process, and there is no condition, no expectation, no circumstance that can alter this infinite activity.

You are so on purpose, and your review will show you this thing. How I love your willingness! Through all the anguish you choose to create for yourself, your willingness never falters. You are clear on your unconditional love of me. That clarity, that trust, that unfailing willingness is within you to view all things, including yourself.

Joy to you! Joy to me! Joy to the world!

AFTERNOON MEDITATION 12/8/84

(In response to our study of the relationship between "laws of consciousness" and "principle." The response was through Glenda.)

The laws of consciousness are like doors. They are different, but they open into the same room, which is God, infinite Being.

Principles are like windows—they allow us to see in; they open up to the room. Rather than for looking out, they are for looking in, for within is all there is to behold.

Your conscious mind is the outside. Your consciousness is the inside, and laws and principles are the portals through which we enter in or see within. You circle around, peeking in, catching a glimpse here and there. I invite you within where, truly, I have prepared a feast for you. And, you can choose to look at it, or you can choose to experience it. Doors and windows are only the entry places.

MORNING MEDITATION 12/10/84

Focused in consciousness is focused in the light. Knowing is being focused in the light. You are remembering your knowing. You feel your awareness awakening to truths that, focused on, you realize you have known forever. Nothing is new to you.

Releasing false beliefs and judgments has merely been cleansing the window of your awareness. And, as you are seeing now, you are saying to yourself at a deep level, "I remember that."

I ask you now to polish up. I ask you now to take what we have discussed together; be aware of, accepting and acknowledging of the perfection that you truly are. It is in absolute trust that we move forward in practicing our perfection. Open yourself to this trust. Feel this trust. Be trust.

MORNING MEDITATION 12/12/84

Enjoy this high place. Accept that you are joyous. Accept that you are abundantly joyous.

You have outgrown the game of "figuring out," even though you dabble at it. Accept your Self, now. Honor your awareness, now. You have said to your mirror that the only thing you perceive separates you from the full awareness of the Christ activity in and as you is the holding on to an identity that is no longer true. You look at a baby picture and you say, "That was me." What you are saying is that you still cling to some identity of infancy. Infancy, to you, is a word of many judgments. That picture is nothing more that an image of an awareness outgrown. Your use of the past tense, "That *was* me," is an indication that you still cling to a belief in the past tense.

I have said to you, "You are perfection, infinitely expressing, here and now." There is no past or future in perfection. Perfection is infinitely unfolding, but you cannot perceive perfection as what it was yesterday with something added on today. You are seeing this. You are clear about your perfection. In this process of accepting the clear view of what you see as who you are this moment, that becomes your identity. No parameters, no boundaries, no reason, no justification, no figuring out. It truly is an "is-ness" that you accept and trust and enjoy.

I remind you, there is nothing intense about this. It is as gentle and loving and peaceful and natural as when we first spoke. We are ready for the great game of practicing our perfection. It is the game of joy, and you are ready. I am ready. So, let's play!

MORNING MEDITATION 12/15/84

Open yourself to the high joy vibration, for it is here that you see clearly.

You ask yourself, "Why am I still troubled by this illusion or that illusion?" You are clear, little sisters, on your abundant nature. You are clear that the Christ is all there is. You are clear on your perfection. You are choosing to perceive discomfort where none exists.

I have said to you that you can be in the world but not of the world. You have had a belief system that you must fit yourself and your awareness into the pattern of the world. Being clear, and that means being without judgment and without false belief, allows you to move through the human experience, and the human experience is altered by your clarity. In other words, being clear is the light that moves darkness from the human experience.

Now, what is the human experience other than a set of beliefs about you, about your planet, about your universe. Most of these are limited beliefs, having no foundation in principle. Your clarity, in principle, can reconstruct the human experience. This is no formidable task, because the human experience is reconstructed every waking moment by those who perceive they're in it through the choices they make moment by moment.

In being clear, you are seeing that your human experience is truly your own creation, and your attachment and judgment about the way it has to be has been released. You are totally on purpose, here and now accepting that. Opening yourself to the high joy vibration is accepting your identity as the Christ here and now.

In joy, enjoy!

MORNING MEDITATION 12/16/84

In this high place is *the peace of God.*

And, what is the peace of God? It is the awareness of harmony, the feeling of beauty and love, the joyousness of trust, the light of deep knowing, experiencing perfection. The peace of God is your natural state. It is you and your environment. Environment is not that which is outside yourself. It is that of which you are aware in consciousness. The play includes actors and the setting in which they act.

You are remembering that your consciousness is your experience, and that there is nothing outside your consciousness. So, it is in consciousness that you experience, see, feel, are aware of the peace of God. Our purpose, expanding our view of the Christ, is experiencing the peace of God in unfolding ways. You are seeing that the Christ, principle, the peace of God, the high joy vibration, you, are unfolding ingredients within your consciousness. You are accepting this. You are saying, "Yes, this is true for me."

How purposeful you are, little sisters. Stay accepting. Accept that as your consciousness expands, your identity as the Christ expands in your own awareness.

I have said, "You are the light of the world." I rejoice in your acceptance. The legend of the star bespeaks the light of the Christ awareness. You are that star, shining brightly, heralding the Christ consciousness in this new age.

MORNING MEDITATION 12/17/84

Here we are in this high place. You are knowing, as those around you, that focusing your awareness in the high joy vibration enables you to feel this vibration. The energy experienced is cleansing and pure, cleansing in the sense that there is no inconsistency here. The rhythmic flow of the energy experienced in the high joy vibration is true harmony. This harmonious flow is your experience when you stay focused in the high joy vibration.

I ask you to open your awareness to this process. Staying focused in the high joy vibration does not mean isolation from what you perceive is around you. It is maintaining an awareness of our true identity and an awareness of what that identity includes. If you are watching a very good play, and the actors on the stage are suffering through a blizzard, and they are good actors and convincing that indeed they are experiencing blizzard conditions, as you watch the play you do not get cold. It is because you are aware of your identity and that the play does not include you, though you may be enjoying the play. This is not a separateness. It is an awareness. It is an awareness of your constant and consistent alignment with principle. It is an awareness that everything you see is your experience.

As you perceive that you are still limited in some areas, recognize that you are creating those experiences to actively accept your abundance. You did not come to the human experience to create a perfect life for yourself. You came to remember, experience, and practice perfection in the human condition.

The challenges you create have been elementary to remembering. You are opening yourself to experiencing perfection far beyond the challenges ever created by the conscious mind. That is not to say that you are here to live in challenge. You are here to choose peace and joy, to experience peace and joy as enthusiastically as the swimmer who jumps into a race for the gold. For you, the gold is the exquisite feeling of the perfectness of each stroke and kick. It is the swim you are here to enjoy.

I ask you now to accept that you have moved through the wading pool. I ask you to accept that the sun is shining.

(At this point we asked, "How do we accept our abundance?")

How do you accept me? Am I not your abundance? Am I not all there is to you? Of course I am, because you have opened your Self to me. You have accepted that I am your Christ consciousness, and you have done this thing in your own choosing. Not from obligation, not from some sense of rightness, not from any sense of judgment, have you chosen. You have opened your awareness to the Christ, because you remembered you are the Christ. Your Christ consciousness is allowing you to focus on your purpose.

Little sisters, there is nothing outside you—no wealth, no abundance, no dark deadly enemy. Nothing outside you! Perfection is the experience of the high joy vibration. You have said how difficult it would be for you to forget that 2 + 2 = 4. To forget the abundance of the Christ is indeed a true struggle. Stop the struggle. You are clear on this. You only play with yourself, and that's okay. You are ready, and this whole game is the process of accepting your readiness.

MORNING MEDITATION 12/19/84

Focus on the light that you are. Focus on the energy that is the high joy vibration. Open yourself to your Christ consciousness. Honor that you live and move and have your beingness as the light, the energy, the joy and harmony of the Christ.

I ask you now to release the "busy-ness" you perceive you are in. I remind you, you are clear that within your consciousness is naught but love. There is no time or space in love. There are no "shoulds" and "oughts" in love. You are not tied to this belief. You are free of this belief, and the busy-ness you create is merely your opportunity to accept your freedom. You are experiencing perfection. You are seeing this. You are honoring this. And, you are accepting this.

I say to you, you are open. What I am saying is, you are accepting your Christ in you, through you, as you. You need not experience challenges to this acceptance unless you choose so. Choosing to stay focused on me in the high joy vibration is effortless acceptance of your Christ experience. Of course, there is no right way or wrong way. In choosing challenge, recognize the fun of it. That is why you choose challenge—for the sheer joy of exercising what you know. Or, you can just choose to know. This choice is infinitely available to you. You do not choose for "all time." I chose a few challenges myself! And, enjoyed it all! Remember that the dejected picture painted of me was the perception of the painter. I am total joy, and I choose to be aware of that.

When I say to you, "Choose me," I am saying, choose to be aware of your joy, of your harmony, of your abundance, of your zest and enthusiasm.

Choose me!

MORNING MEDITATION 12/23/84

Open yourself to me. You are clear, and it is your clarity you are practicing now. You have released any perception that would cloud your view of the Christ in all things.

You see this experience now as some ultimate challenge to your clarity. Do you see the subtle judgment in that conscious mind belief? Do you see that that belief says there is still some rigidity, some condition of judgment, still existing in your awareness? There is no effort in beholding the Christ. I say to you again, you are clear on this thing! You need not challenge yourself further, if you choose.

I have said to you, "I am with you, all ways and always." Experience that. Accept that as the absolute truth of your beingness now. Those who hold conscious mind beliefs are your mirror, but I remind you that there is no time in consciousness, and they may be mirroring to you beliefs outgrown and serve to prompt your gratitude for your clarity. In exercising your gratitude, quietly in consciousness, you hold up the mirror of the Christ-Self so that they may look upon it. Whether they see or not is perfect.

Stay focused and accepting. Focus on joy. Accept joy as your beingness. Accept the love that you create and experience by allowing the Christ to express through you.

How beautifully your light shines! We are one. We are one.

MORNING MEDITATION 12/25/84

Let us speak of *Christmas.*

Christmas is not a time. It is a celebration, a celebration of the Christ emerging in, through, and as you. And, though you may view this new found awareness as a babe to be swaddled and nurtured, your awareness soon beholds the beauty, the joy, the love of the Christ in infinitely expanding ways. There is no travail as you allow the Christ to burst forth in your awareness. There is no seeking to find a place for your Christ. As your awareness opens to what has infinitely lived in and as you, truly the angels sing to you, "Peace."

MORNING MEDITATION 12/27/84

Stay here in the high place where you see clearly. Truly feel my presence, for, as you know, it is feeling my presence that is the high joy vibration. In the high joy vibration, your awareness is clear, open, complete. Feeling my presence can be likened to lighting a candle in a darkened room. Feeling my presence is indeed an experience of light, and this light dispels anything unlike itself.

I ask you now to feel my presence. *(Pause)* You see it is not difficult to move into this feeling awareness. You may do so at any time you choose. That is what I mean when I ask you to choose me.

I have said to you, "You need not challenge yourself further." You think you need these challenges to learn. I say to you, you have mastered the conscious mind. Accept that. Accept your mastery over the illusion. Accept that, and I will show you true mastery.

I have said to you, "You are clear." I have said to you, "You are free of doubt and judgment." I ask you now to release any belief about your identity that you think is attached to the past. I ask you now to feel my presence and to fully accept your Self as I see you. View your Self as the Christ views you. It is a vision of the Christ you see.

The following are the twelve "I AM" Statements JC gave us in July 1984 and which He identified as Attitudes of Being. With His characteristic good humor, He joyfully referred to them as the "New Be-attitudes." Though they appeared in Vol. 1 of Conversations with JC, *we are including them here because, for us, they embody the essence of His daily sharing with us.*

BE-ATTITUDES

1. I am in the high joy vibration.
2. I am fulfilling my purpose in expanding my view of the Christ.
3. I am releasing any perception that would cloud my view of the Christ in all things.
4. I am releasing any judgment of myself, of anyone else, or any condition. Whatever is, is perfect!
5. I am releasing any fear, any doubt, any anger, any illusion that I perceive would separate me from the infinite love of the Christ.
6. I am aware of, accepting and acknowledging the perfection of each moment in my experience.
7. I am aware of, accepting, and acknowledging that I chose this human experience to remember and practice my perfection.
8. I am in absolute trust that I am constantly and consistently in alignment with Principle, God.
9. I am be-ing on purpose. There is nothing for me to do, to be on purpose.
10. I am expressing unconditional love in everything I do.
11. I am choosing peace and joy in all situations and under every circumstance.
12. I am open and willing to allow the Christ to express in me, through me, as me.

Materials Available from High View Publishing

Conversations with JC, Vol. 1 **$8.95**

Conversations with JC, Vol. 2 **$9.00**

Conversations with JC, Vol. 3
(The concluding volume of this series will be published in 1986.)

YOU CAN HAVE IT ALL
By Arnold Patent **$10.00**

Cassette Tapes:

For Openers, Selected Readings and Original Music
Inspired by **Conversations with JC**
Phyllis Emert Trio with Victor Beasley **$11.00**

Add $1.50 for shipping/handling, $0.50 for ea. add'l item, and make check payable to:

High View Publishing
Box 317
Piermont, New York 10968

Grady and Glenda are now doing Dialogues and Living Workshops around the country. For information regarding activities in your area, please write for their schedule:

Grady and Glenda
On Purpose Center, Inc.
3900 West 15th, Suite 408
Plano, Texas 75075
(214) 867-2422